The Pourcel Brothers

Cookbook

MANAGING EDITORS: Stephen Bateman
and Pierre-Jean Furet

EDITOR:
Brigitte Éveno

ART DIRECTOR:
Florence Cailly (China)

PRODUCTION: Claire Leleu

©2003 HACHETTE LIVRE
(Hachette Pratique – Hachette Practical Books)

This edition first published in English in 2004 by Hachette
Illustrated UK, Octopus Publishing Group Ltd., 2–4 Heron Quays,
London E14 4JP
English translation © Octopus Publishing Group Ltd.

Translation from French: First Edition Translations Ltd., in
conjunction with Book Production Consultants plc, Cambridge

ISBN-13: 978-1-84430-124-9
ISBN-10: 1-84430-124-9

Jacques & Laurent Pourcel

Pourcel Brothers
Cookbook

our recipes from La Compagnie des Comptoirs

Photographs: Bernhard Winkelmann

Stylist: Valérie Lhomme

Project editor: Philippe Lamboley

Editorial associate: Sophie Brissaud

HACHETTE Illustrated

Contents

Introduction

Roots in Languedoc

How do you know where you belong when you're from the Western part of the French Mediterranean South?

You can stay right there and get to know the intricate details of your own country; you can learn, from two sips of wine, how to tell grapes from one patch of a Languedocian vineyard from the next one; you can spot the local thyme and sage in the fragrance of a picpoul rosé; love both the quiet, wide-open sandy seaside between Camargue and Catalonia and the white, sun-baked, windswept limestone heights of a goat-ridden, gamey hinterland, where chestnuts and cèpe mushrooms grow; you can sharpen your senses of smell and taste, anticipating the truffle season, around November. Simply, you can just let yourself be from Languedoc. We know how to do this, but we have also learned that the further away you travel from your origins, the clearer and more precise they appear to you at a distance. Since we have entered the world of haute cuisine and the status of star-chefdom, we have been constantly navigating between these two poles: our Southern French roots and the call of faraway destinations. Perhaps because we are twin brothers we find no contradiction in this dichotomy. Being two allows us sometimes to be twice as strong as one would be, and sometimes to be like one person in two different places.

So we let our dreams take us along the coast

Above and left: *laticed shutters, golden colors and culinary escape in Montpellier and La Grande-Motte.*

Right: *the restaurant in Montpellier, created and opened in 2000, marked the beginning of La Compagnie des Comptoirs.*

and across the sea, through Spain to Africa, and via Greece and Turkey to the Middle and Far East; such is the natural impulse of being born in Languedoc, close to the antique seaports of Marseille, Agde, Sète and Barcelona: the South calls you. Our region is like a balcony which opens out onto the sea, and allows your imagination to take in the whole Mediterranean in a wide fan-shaped movement. Marseille offers it all in a nutshell, with a plentiful North African population coloring and shaping the city's culture and destiny, as Greek, Roman and Spanish settlers have done long before them. Beyond Spain, Italy and the three countries of Maghreb – Morocco, Algeria and Tunisia – lies the East of North Africa, the West of Asia and the many Greek islands which appear like stepping-stones to the East. For thousands of years, this region has been a melting pot, a cultural and commercial community, a combination of tastes, colors and smells that form the character of the Mediterranean cuisines. This is our natural element; a little mobility was all it took to grasp it fully. Following that movement, it was easy to take the dream further: to India, Southeast Asia, China and Japan.

We belong both here and there. We are not affiliated to any school and do not feel tied down by tradition or past influences. We prefer to be ourselves, to look towards the future; Mediterranean at heart, but something different as well.

La Compagnie des Comptoirs in France

Since we and our friend and associate, Olivier Château, created our first gourmet restaurant *Le Jardin des Sens* in 1988, we have constantly promoted the produce and the cuisine of our region, although other regions – the Mediterranean, Asia, the Indian Ocean islands – have obviously influenced our cooking as well. However, we felt a strong desire to explore the world, and after our restaurant *Le Jardin des Sens* received its third Michelin star, in 1997, this exploration began to take shape as with the formation of *La Compagnie des Comptoirs* and the opening of new restaurants in France and abroad.

La Compagnie des Comptoirs is the embodiment of three ideas that we cherish. The first is to travel with your mind and senses through the cuisine and culture of a region. Second is to gather people in a pleasant, relaxed, modern, relatively inexpensive place, where you serve them delicious food and make them happy (an echo of our own natural sense of friendship and conviviality). Third is a fascination with the exotic culture of colonial

Europe, the spice trade between West and East Indies, the Far East, the Indian Ocean, the South Seas, the New World. It is the convergence of many desires into one single aim: making good cooking more fun, more accessible, and a better stimulant for the imagination.

The first *Compagnie des Comptoirs* was created in December 2000, in Montpellier, facing *Le Jardin des Sens*. We asked the interior designer Imaad Rahmouni – who follows us through every new *Compagnie* – to produce a warm atmosphere, both modern and timeless, with exotic woods, carved Indonesian screens, antique sea maps, leather-bound books and etchings from colonial histories, like a sensorial echo of the East India Company. Outside the restaurant, a large patio is centered around a water pond, a feature that all *Compagnies des Comptoirs* have in common.

The concept of the *Compagnies* also extends itself to the food: generous, light, colorful and inspired by the East and the South – but mostly through a constant renewing of our imagination – it is meant to provoke satisfaction and excitement at a moderate price. One year later, a second *Compagnie* was created in Avignon, in the extraordinary setting of an 18th-century convent. We decided to give this place a more modern look than that of the first *Compagnie*. Soon afterwards, with the third *Compagnie*, *Effet*

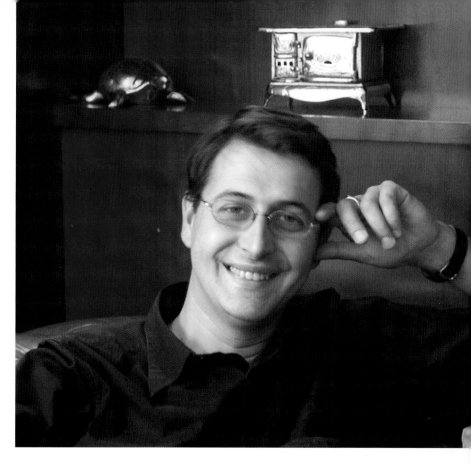

Mer – on the coast near Montpellier – we renewed the concept of the beach restaurant. *Effet Mer* is a long structure divided into several rooms and lounges by carved teakwood panels, and shaded by a huge sand-colored awnings. With your feet in the sand while you are eating or having a drink, the sense of the tropical East is ever present in the sea wind that gently plays through the saffron-colored awnings of Balinese four-posted beds and the palm trees and cacti of a seashore garden.

While *La Compagnie des Comptoirs* is our poetic venture into the concept of travel, our cuisine has been doing some real travelling. Soon after the first *Compagnie* opened in Montpellier, our brasserie *Sens et Saveurs* opened above the Tokyo Imperial Gardens. Spring 2004 saw the opening of another one

Left: *Jacques and Laurent Pourcel.*

Above:
Olivier Château, Jacques and Laurent Pourcel's partner.

11

Above:
Effet Mer is a long buiding divided into separate rooms by teak partitions, and shaded by a large sand colored awning.

of our restaurants in Bangkok, followed by a further opening in Shanghai in Autumn 2004. We remain particularly fond of all our *Compagnies*, in which we put a lot of ourselves and some of our most cherished principles.

W!Sens, the *Compagnie* in London

Our travels have taken us primarily to the South and East. By comparison, we got to know Northern Europe rather late. To us, London was a gradual discovery, over the last few years. From one short visit to another, we took a liking to this beautiful metropolis. What we found there was not only the capital of England but indeed the whole world, contained in one large, lively city. The combination of the British lifestyle – with its passion for comfort, peacefulness and elegance – and the cosmopolitan culture inherited from the former colonial empire fascinated us right from the start. While it is as beautiful as its near neighbor Paris, in London everything is on a more human scale and it is buzzing with life.

The street culture, the theatres, museums and galleries, and of course the food and wine: in London, wherever you stand, there is always something to do, to see, to taste, to share; something new and exciting around the corner. Cafés, restaurants, theatres are all brimming with vitality and creativity. We greatly enjoy this openness, youthfulness and diversity, particularly in the culinary field. In London, you may taste excellent and genuine ethnic foods – Chinese, Indian, Thai, Japanese, West Indian – and in gourmet cuisine and British food, many new and talented local chefs have reinstated, during the last decade, London's worldwide reputation as a city of fine eating.

The creation of a new *Compagnie des Comptoirs* in London seemed to us like a logical decision. Some of our British clients in Montpellier and Avignon urged us to open a *Compagnie* in London, we finally followed

their advice and made the move. The concept of the *Compagnie* seems particularly well suited to the cosmopolitan, pleasure-loving and lively atmosphere of London. No translation is necessary between the Languedocian South, dreaming of Mediterranean and Oriental escapades, and London, open and welcoming to people from all directions and from all nations. For *W'Sens*, we adapted the concept of *La Compagnie des Comptoirs* to a whole new environment and clientele. The restaurant is located in an elegant building in beautiful Waterloo Place, part of the historical heart of London. It has a total area of 800 square meters on three levels. In accordance with the concept of *La Compagnie des Comptoirs*, there is a lounge bar on the ground floor, where the main dining-room is also located and a large staircase leading to a mezzanine. Once again, we asked Imaad Rahmouni to design this venue, with a stress on timelessness and memorabilia of colonial splendor. We want this décor to last for years, knowing that what is fashionable today will be out of fashion tomorrow.

The menu, predictably, reflects the fourfold concept of the *Compagnie*: Vegetables, the South, the East, and Desserts. Through our choice of dishes, we are trying to reach and satisfy the widest possible audience. And we are confident that Londoners will love to travel with us to the colorful regions of taste that we

have already had so much fun exploring.

W'SENS
By La Compagnie des Comptoirs
12 Waterloo Place
St James's
London
SW1

www.lacompagniedescomptoirs.com

Opposite page, top Left: *vaulted ceilings and pale stone in this ancient 17th century cloister, which since 2001 has housed La Compagnie des Comptoirs in Avignon.*

bottom right: *Exterior of W'Sens, La Compagnie des Comptoirs in the heart of London.*

Twelve early summer vegetables, herb dressing, and crushed peanuts

For cooking the vegetables
1 piece fresh ginger
1 piece fresh galangal
1 dried chile pepper (optional)
2 cups cold water
7 tbsp grapeseed oil
2¼ sticks/9 oz unsalted butter
juice of 1 lime
salt

Early summer vegetables
4 "petals" of slow-baked tomato (see recipe on p. 54)
2 baby violet artichokes
4 spears of green asparagus
4 red radishes
2 large, bulbous scallions
2 baby zucchini
4 cauliflower florets
1 stalk celery
2 very small, young bulbs of fennel
½ Chinese cabbage (Chinese leaves)
¾ cup baby fava beans, shucked, inner skins removed
8 snow-peas

To assemble the dish
A few leaves each of fresh Thai basil, chives, and mint
Toasted, crushed peanuts

Peel the ginger and the galangal. Finely chop the ginger; mince or grate the galangal. Crumble the dried chile pepper.

Cooking the vegetables

Set the tomato petals aside for garnishing the finished dish. Peel and wash all the vegetables as appropriate and cut them into small, differently shaped pieces. Cook each type separately (except for the fava beans and snow-peas) in approximately ¼ cup water with ½ teaspoon grapeseed oil, a little ginger, galingal and chile pepper, 1–2 teaspoons butter, and a pinch of salt for each batch.

Add a squeeze of lime juice to the water in which you cook the artichokes and the celery. Cook the fava beans and the snow-peas separately, in boiling, salted water, as directed for the green vegetables at the top of facing page, page 19, until they are tender but still crisp. Plunge into iced water to refresh so they will keep their color; drain.

Assembling the dish

Drain off the flavored cooking juices from all the vegetables (see note on page 20 at end of recipe) and reserve in a bowl. Keep hot. Arrange all the vegetables on fairly deep plates or shallow soup dishes; decorate each serving with a tomato petal. Add more flavor if needed to the reserved cooking juices, using grapeseed oil, salt, and lime juice. Use an electric whisk to blend this dressing; add the fresh herb leaves. Sprinkle over the vegetables. Top with a sprinkling of coarsely chopped or crushed peanuts.

This dish, with its echoes of Thailand, is prepared in much the same way as the Greek vegetable salad on page 20, but the two recipes use very different spices and flavors, giving a choice between Mediterranean and Asian interpretations of mixed-vegetable salads.

Vegetable medley on puff pastry base with pesto and black olive vinaigrette

Cooking the vegetables

Clean and prepare all the vegetables. Cook each type separately in boiling water until tender but still crisp, allowing scant 2 tablespoons salt per 4 cups water for the green vegetables (snow-peas, asparagus, green beans) and 1 tablespoon salt per 4 cups water for the other vegetables (carrots, turnips, scallions, artichokes). Drain each batch of vegetables and plunge into a large bowl of ice water to refresh and "fix" the color.

Cooking the puff pastry

Preheat the oven to 425 °F. Roll out the pastry into a thin sheet and use a cookie cutter to cut out 4 rounds of the required size, according to preference, and use the prongs of a fork to prick the surface of the pastry. Transfer to a prepared baking sheet; place a second, matching baking sheet on top of the pastry rounds and bake for 12 minutes in the oven. Halfway through this time, remove the top baking sheet and allow the pastry to finish baking and turn pale golden brown. Set aside.

Pesto dressing

Place the basil leaves, the garlic cloves, olive oil, and a little salt in a food processor or blender. Process until smoothly blended. Transfer to a bowl and clean the food processor or blender, ready to make the black olive dressing.

Tapenade (black olive) dressing

Place all the ingredients for this in the blender or food processor and process at high speed. Adjust seasoning to taste.

Assembling the dish

Reheat all the vegetables together with a little olive oil in a heavy-bottomed pan or casserole dish; when they have reheated, add a generous tablespoon of pesto and stir; season with salt and pepper to taste.

Spoon a little pesto into a saucer and roll the cherry tomatoes in it.

Reheat the pastry rounds gently for a few minutes and place one in the center of each of 4 plates. Spread a little tapenade over each pastry round, then arrange one-quarter of the vegetables on top; decorate with a pesto-flavored tomato. Garnish each serving with a few arugula leaves. Dribble a thread of pesto around the outer edge of the pastry; repeat this last process with the black olive dressing.

> This is another recipe that makes the most of our Mediterranean repertoire (the flavors of pesto and tapenade are typical of this region), providing a medley of sun-drenched tastes heaped on crisp and tender flaky pastry.

To serve 4

1 packet ready-made puff pastry

For the vegetable medley
4 oz baby carrots
4 oz baby turnips
3½ oz snow-peas
4 oz large scallions
5 oz green asparagus
3 oz baby violet artichokes
3 oz green beans
sea salt

For the pesto
leaves from a large bunch of fresh basil
3 or 4 cloves of garlic, peeled
1 cup olive oil
salt

For the tapenade (black olive) dressing
9 oz canned black olives, stoned
4 tbsp capers (in vinegar)
1 or 2 cloves of garlic, peeled
⅔ cup olive oil
4 salted anchovies
salt, freshly ground pepper

To assemble the dish
olive oil
4 ripe red cherry tomatoes
3½ oz arugula, rinsed and dried in a cloth
salt, freshly ground pepper

Greek mixed vegetable salad, dried orange zest marinade, sugar-glazed orange slices

To serve 4

For the dried orange
1 cup water
scant ¾ cup sugar
1 orange for the sugar-glazed
orange slices
1 orange for the baked peel

For the vegetables
2 baby carrots
2 white button mushrooms
½ small celery root
4 thin, green asparagus
spears
2 thin baby leeks
2 baby turnips
2 baby fennel bulbs
2 baby zucchini
2 baby globe artichokes
4 cauliflower florets
2 oz fresh chanterelle
mushrooms
8 small snow-pea pods
6 cups water or fresh
chicken stock
scant ½ cup olive oil
salt, whole coriander seeds
1 lemon

**For the Greek-style
dressing**
olive oil
juice of 2 lemons
juice of 1 orange
salt, freshly ground pepper

To assemble the dish
4 slow-baked tomato "petals"
(see recipe on p. 54)
4 very small bunches of fresh
basil

Rinse, peel, and trim all the vegetables as appropriate and cut them into small, differently shaped pieces.

Sugar-glazed orange slices
Make a sugar syrup by bringing the sugar and water to a boil. Use a mandoline cutter or a very sharp knife to cut an unpeeled orange into very thin, round slices. Add these to the sugar syrup and simmer gently for 1 hour. When they are nearly done, preheat the oven to 225 °F.
Drain the orange slices (keep the syrup). Cover a baking sheet with nonstick wax or silicone paper; spread out the orange slices on it in a single layer and dry out in the oven for 1 hour 20 minutes. They should become as crunchy as chips.
Use a potato peeler to peel off the zest of the orange (just the peel, no white pith). Simmer the strips of zest in the reserved sugar syrup for 1 hour, then drain well and spread out on fresh nonstick wax or silicone paper to dry out in the oven, following the method used for the orange slices. When the zest has completely dried out, transfer to the food processor and process to a powder. Set aside.

Cooking the vegetables
With the exception of the snow-peas, cook all the vegetables separately, using ½ cup water or chicken stock, ½ teaspoon olive oil, a pinch of salt, and a few coriander seeds for each batch, until they are tender but still crisp. Do not drain. Sprinkle a little lemon juice over the baby turnips, the artichokes, chanterelles, and celery root. Set aside.

Cook the snow-peas in salted water until tender but crisp, in fast-boiling water (allow scant 2 tablespoons salt for each 4 cups water). Drain and refresh in ice water to "set" their color.

Greek dressing
Drain all the cooked vegetables, pouring their cooking liquid (not that from the snow-peas) into a bowl. Mix this liquid with a little more olive oil and add salt, freshly ground pepper, and lemon and orange juice to taste.

Assembling the dish
Arrange a similar selection of vegetables on each of 4 fairly deep dishes or in shallow soup plates, decorating each serving with a tomato "petal."
Sprinkle each portion with some of the orange zest powder and with the dressing; decorate with a crunchy orange round and with a very small bunch of fresh basil.

> When cooking each type of vegetable, do not allow the liquid to boil dry but merely to reduce. When the reduced cooking juices are mixed together, they will form the Greek-style dressing. There is nothing to stop you varying this recipe, choosing other vegetables, increasing or decreasing the quantity of something or other...

Crisp-fried wonton skins layered with stir-fried vegetables, herb-flavored oil

For the mushroom sauce
scant ½ cup sugar
½ cup rice wine vinegar
(see note in method)
7 oz fresh shiitake
mushrooms, cleaned and
trimmed
2 cups vegetable stock
salt

For the herb-flavored oil
small bunch fresh chives
small bunch fresh cilantro
scant ½ cup olive oil
salt

For the vegetables
5½–6 oz Chinese leaves
(Chinese cabbage)
5–6 oz pak choy (see note at
end of method)
7 oz fresh shiitake
mushrooms
8 oz carrots
2 medium-sized onions
1½ oz fresh ginger, peeled
1 clove garlic, peeled
generous 1 tbsp sesame seed
oil
salt, freshly ground pepper

To assemble the dish
1 packet Chinese wonton
skins (thin pastry squares,
see note at end of method)
4 cups peanut oil for frying

Mushroom sauce

Pour the sugar into a heavy-bottomed pan and cook gently without adding any water until it melts and caramelizes. When it is golden brown, pour in the rice wine vinegar and bring to a boil. Add the shiitake mushrooms, followed by the vegetable stock. Cover and leave to simmer for 45 minutes, then transfer to the blender and process, adding seasoning if necessary. Pour into a pan and keep warm.

Herb-flavored oil

Rinse and dry the chives and cilantro. Take the leaves off the cilantro stalks and process both herbs with the olive oil and a little salt in the blender. Pour into a bowl.

The vegetables

Cut the Chinese cabbage, the pak choy, and the shiitake mushrooms into fairly large pieces; slice the carrots thinly at an angle of 45° (on the slant) and chop the onions finely. Crush the ginger and the garlic or mince very finely indeed. Pour the sesame seed oil into a large fireproof casserole dish or wok and, when hot, add the vegetables; stir-fry over a high heat until they are tender but still very crisp. Add a little mushroom sauce before setting aside.

Assembling the dish

Heat the peanut oil in a deep fryer to a temperature of 325 °F. Fry the wonton skins until they are crisp and pale golden brown; remove from the oil and drain on paper towels.

Place a fried wonton skin on each plate, heap some vegetables on it, cover with another wonton skin and surround with a ribbon of mushroom sauce. Sprinkle a little herb-flavored oil over the top wonton skin.

> You will find all the ingredients you need for this recipe (the vegetables, rice wine vinegar, sesame seed oil, wonton skins etc.) in a good Oriental grocery store or in the better supermarkets. Pak choy or bok choy is a type of Chinese cabbage with fleshy white ribs or stalks and green leaves, rather like a small, squat version of silver beet or Swiss chard.

Fluffy oat cakes, braised chanterelle mushrooms, hazelnut oil

For the oat cakes
Preheat the oven to 350 °F.
Bring the milk to a boil with the butter in a pan. Season with salt and pepper; stir in the rolled oats and leave to stand for 20 minutes. When this mixture has cooled and is lukewarm, separate the egg yolks from their whites. Stir the yolks into the oat mixture; whisk the egg whites until they form peaks and fold gently into the oat mixture in a large mixing bowl, using a spatula.
Transfer a quarter of this mixture into each of 4 deep, round, nonstick molds 3 inches in diameter (dariole molds are ideal); the molds should be three-quarters full. Bake for approximately 30 minutes in the oven, then turn out and keep hot.

Braised chanterelles
Clean the chanterelles. Heat the butter in a heavy-bottomed pan and sauté the chanterelles briefly over a high heat. Season with salt and pepper and drain in a strainer placed over the bowl; keep the juices. Return this juice to the pan and cook, uncovered, until it has reduced to a thicker, syrupy consistency. Beat in the hazelnut oil with a hand-held electric whisk. Keep warm.

Herb salad
Pick over the herbs, rinse them and blot dry. Make the vinaigrette by mixing the salt and pepper with the vinegar, then add the hazelnut oil in a thin stream while beating energetically. Sprinkle a little of this dressing over the herbs just before assembling the dish.

Assembling the dish
Place an oat cake in the center of each plate. Top each oat cake with some chanterelles (make sure these are really hot), then place some of the mixed-herb salad on top. Surround with a narrow trace of vinaigrette and with a separate ring of the reduced mushroom cooking liquid.

> The taste of the rolled oats goes perfectly with that of the hazelnut oil, and the chanterelles add a woodland note. Do not use too much of the hazelnut oil as it has a very strong taste.

To serve 4

For the oat cakes
2½ cups milk
1½ sticks/6 oz butter
1½ cups rolled oats (not the instant variety)
6 eggs
salt, freshly ground pepper

For the braised chanterelle mushrooms
8 oz fresh chanterelle mushrooms
3 tbsp butter
1 tbsp hazelnut oil
salt, freshly ground pepper

For the herb salad
3½ oz young, tender herbs (chervil, flat-leaf parsley, chives, arugula)
½ tbsp sherry vinegar
2 tbsp hazelnut oil
salt, freshly ground pepper

Vegetarian foods and vegetables

Chanterelle mushrooms, cream of artichokes, artichoke chips, and walnut oil

To serve 4

For the cream of Jerusalem artichokes and chips
1–1¼ lb Jerusalem artichokes
1 mild white onion
½ stick/2 oz unsalted butter
4 cups chicken stock
1 cup light cream
4 cups oil for frying
salt, freshly ground white pepper

For the purée of flatleaf parsley
1 large bunch flatleaf parsley
½ medium-sized, mild white onion
Scant ½ cup crème fraîche or whole milk yogurt (see note after method on p. 116)
salt, freshly ground white pepper

For the sautéed chanterelle mushrooms
12 oz fresh chanterelle mushrooms
½ stick/2 oz unsalted butter
salt, freshly ground pepper

For the dressing
2 tbsp walnut oil

Cream of Jerusalem artichokes

Peel the artichokes with a potato peeler. Rinse them and blot dry. Reserve 2 of the most regular-shaped artichokes; cut the rest into fairly large pieces. Peel the onion and slice into thin rings.

Heat the butter in a heavy-bottomed pan, add the onion and cook gently until tender but not browned at all. Add the artichokes and the chicken stock; boil gently for approximately 30 minutes, or until the artichokes are very tender. Once they are done, add the cream, bring back to boiling point, and then liquidize in the blender or food processor until smooth. Add salt and pepper to taste.

Jerusalem artichoke chips

Cut the 2 remaining artichokes lengthwise into very thin slices (use a mandoline cutter or a very sharp knife) and deep-fry in the hot oil (325 °F) until they are golden brown and crisp. Remove from the oil and drain on paper towels, sprinkle with salt and keep hot, uncovered.

Purée of flatleaf parsley

Use only the leaves of the parsley (removing all the stalks) and rinse. To "set" the color, blanch in a pan of boiling salted water, allowing scant 2 tablespoons salt for each 4 cups water, then drain and immediately rinse under the cold faucet; blot dry in a clean cloth. Cut the onion into small dice. Heat the crème fraîche or yogurt and the onion in an uncovered pan and simmer until reduced and thickened considerably. Process the reduced crème fraîche or yogurt, the onion, and the blanched parsley leaves in the blender or food processor until very smooth; season with salt and pepper.

Sautéed chanterelle mushrooms

Clean and trim the mushrooms, rinse briefly under the cold faucet, drain well. Heat the butter in a skillet and sauté the mushrooms until they are lightly browned (about 10 minutes). Season with salt and pepper to taste.

Assembling the dish

On each of 4 heated shallow soup plates or fairly deep dishes, place one-quarter of the mushroom mixture; in the center of this place a spoonful of the parsley purée, garnish with artichoke chips, and surround with a very thin ribbon of walnut oil. Use a hand-held electric beater to combine the remaining walnut oil with the cream of Jerusalem artichoke soup and serve very hot, in separate bowls.

This spectrum of fall colors and tastes is enhanced by the vivid green of the parsley. Choose small, very fresh chanterelles that will all take the same amount of time to cook; they should still have a little "bite" to them when done.

If you use yogurt in place of crème fraîche, do not use low or nonfat yogurt because this separates when heated.

Fruit and vegetables of the Languedoc

We created a "vegetarian and vegetable" menu for the Compagnie des Comptoirs, not in response to current fashion, but because we are passionate about the vegetables of the Languedoc-Roussillon region in southern France. The lively, light, and versatile nature of these specialties is a secret long shared by the Mediterranean countries. In our part of the world, vegetables have always been valued for themselves and not limited to the role of a mere culinary foil. Far from being the gastronomic self-denial frequently associated with vegetarian cooking, our approach focuses on whole-hearted enjoyment. How could it be otherwise with so many wonderful plants, herbs, and fruits just there for the picking?

In the Languedoc, local produce is all about colors, flavors, and scents. This area epitomizes the south of France, especially westward, toward Perpignan and Roussillon, the Catalan part of the

The wonderful vegetables of southern France benefit from the bright light of Languedoc, flourishing in the heat and sun.
Above: all is ready for lunch on the beach, in the shaded and peaceful surroundings of the Compagnie des Comptoir's Effet Mer restaurant.
Left: the reed beds of La Petite Camargue in the Gard.

Below: *an ancient treasure—dating back to biblical times!—of the Mediterranean basin; under the summer sun the olive trees' fruits ripen, ready to produce their liquid gold.*
Right: *the violet or* poivrade *artichoke, one of the jewels of southern cooking, hails from Sicily. Catherine de' Medici loved this flower-cum-vegetable and promoted its cultivation in France.*

country, beyond the River Aude and its wetlands. With the rest of France to the east, Spain to the west, the mountainous Cevennes to the north and the Mediterranean to the south, we can choose from the foods produced in the wooded and rocky uplands, such as wild mushrooms and truffles; goats' or ewes' milk cheeses from the limestone plateaux of the Causses and the Montagne Noire (Black Mountain) area; the fruits of the sea; and all that flourishes on our sandy plains and in our orchards and vegetable plots. We tend our vegetables as if they were jewels.

Treasures from our soil

What other vegetable/fruit embodies the pleasure of living in the Mediterranean region as well as the tomato, with its insatiable appetite for sunlight? Its refreshing sweetness is balm after the heat of the sun. A friend, Roger Maelstaff, is the prince of tomato growers. He cultivates a dozen or so varieties at Pouzols, in the Minervois area, among them the Spanish Moya, enormous and fleshy, one of which is enough for a salad for two; the Andine; the Ananas (or so-called 'pineapple' tomato); the beefsteak tomato; the evergreen… We cannot resist the pleasure of using them raw, in sorbets, in granitas, jellied, as gazpacho, slow-baked in the oven… When we need a meal of nature's fast food, nothing compares with a thickly sliced ripe, red Moya tomato, simply sprinkled

with olive oil and a small amount of good quality sea salt. From the number of recipes we have created using tomatoes, it is obvious how much we love them.

The phrase "vegetables from the South" also calls to mind tender fava beans, asparagus from Mauguio, the most tender baby artichokes, bulbs of fennel, eggplant, and bell peppers. Then there are the salads and herbs with their distinctive full-bodied, aromatic, and sometimes peppery taste. Arugula is one such, said to be hot enough to waken the dead. Basil, chervil, and the first young shoots of spinach may also be found throughout the region, while certain vegetables are the pride of a particular village, such as the black turnips of Pardailhan, grown only on the chalk and slate plateau of Haut-Languedoc. Official recognition in the form of an "appellation d'origine controlée" for this exceptional root vegetable, with its sweetly aromatic and complex taste, is long overdue. The small town of Lézignan-la-Cèbe derives its name from the mild onions (known as cèbes) renowned there since the seventeenth century. They must be eaten while still fresh. The white onions from Citou (Aude), Toulouges (eastern Pyrenees) and those grown in the Cevennes are less perishable and are therefore to be found outside the Languedoc region—and outside France.

The scented fruits of the South

Which fruits should we choose as the most redolently evocative of our region? The first to spring to mind is the apricot. This golden globe with its intoxicating scent and flavor symbolizes the Languedoc-Roussillon, whether it is presented raw, or as a conserve, or preserved in brandy… We love to couple it with almonds and with orgeat, for a typically southern marriage. Hidden in the soil of our hinterland there is another perfumed "fruit": the truffle, a black treasure which is traded in the markets of Uzès, Anduze, and Bagnols-sur-Cèze during the winter months and accounts for approximately 15 percent of the truffle crop in France. Of all Languedoc's fruits, however, the crown must go to the olive! The green *lucques*, the *picholine* pickling olive, the black olives used for making tapenade, and the *negrette* and *verdale* varieties that yield such precious olive oil—from our childhood, the fragrance of olive oil has surrounded us. We use it without thinking, as the air that we breathe, and its pure taste never palls. Whether as seasoning or dressing, combining different flavors or enhancing the simplest dishes, it is fundamental: a golden thread running through our cuisine.

New season's asparagus: cooked à la plancha, raw in a salad, citrus fruits and tomato salsa

For the asparagus

30 green asparagus spears

3 tbsp olive oil

juice of 1 lemon

salt, freshly ground pepper

For the citrus vinaigrette

1 orange

½ pomelo

½ lemon

3 tbsp olive oil

1 slow-baked tomato, diced

(see recipe on p. 54)

small bunch cilantro

salt, freshly ground pepper

To serve

¼ cup Parmesan shavings

Clean the asparagus and peel the lower parts of the stem with a potato peeler or special asparagus peeler, taking care not to damage their tips.

For the citrus vinaigrette

Peel the orange, pomelo, and lemon with a very sharp, pointed serrated knife, removing all the pith. Extract the segments carefully from their thin, white membranes and cut them into fairly small dice. Add the olive oil and the diced slow-baked tomato, and season with salt and freshly ground pepper. Set aside.

For the asparagus

Heat a griddle pan or very wide, heavy skillet, having first brushed the surface with oil; spread 24 asparagus spears out in a single layer and roast over a gentle heat, turning frequently until tender but still crisp. Season with salt and pepper and set aside. Slice the remaining 6 raw asparagus spears lengthwise into very thin strips, using a mandoline or very sharp knife; sprinkle with lemon juice, salt, pepper, and olive oil.

To serve

Finish the preparation of the citrus vinaigrette by stirring in the coarsely snipped cilantro leaves. Arrange 6 roasted asparagus spears in the center of each plate.

Place one-quarter of the raw, dressed spears on top of each serving of roasted asparagus and surround with the citrus vinaigrette. Decorate each portion with one or two Parmesan shavings.

> Asparagus is one of our favorite vegetables and here it is prepared in two different ways for the same dish. The asparagus grown at Mauguio, near Montpellier, is renowned for its quality. Citrus fruit is the perfect complement to bring out the fresh, agreeably sharp, springtime flavor of new season's asparagus. It is unusual to broil or sear vegetables: once you try it, you will be a convert.

Fresh goat's cheeses, roast apricots, spicy layered pastry slices, caramelized Banyuls wine

4 fresh, mild, white goat's cheeses, weighing 3½–4 oz each
3 cups Banyuls wine (natural sweet, French fortified white wine)
olive oil

Spicy layered pastry
1 lb phyllo pastry (see note at end of recipe)
1 stick/4 oz butter, melted
selection of white, black, green, and pink peppercorns (see method)
confectioners' sugar

Roast apricots
6 naturally ripened, best quality apricots
salt, freshly ground pepper

Boil the Banyuls wine in an uncovered pan until it has reduced to a syrupy consistency: it is ready when it lightly coats the bottom of the pan when the pan is tipped to one side. If reduced excessively, the syrup will be bitter. Preheat the oven to 350 °F.
Rinse the apricots, cut them in half, remove their pits and cut into quarters. Set aside.

Spicy layered pastry
Lightly grease a baking sheet with butter and spread a sheet of phyllo out on it. Brush all over the surface with melted butter. Use a pepper mill filled with a selection of the peppercorns to sprinkle lightly with freshly ground pepper mixture. Cover with another sheet of phyllo, brush this in turn with butter and sprinkle again with pepper mixture. Repeat until you have 4 layers of pastry sheets, sprinkling the last sheet with a light dusting of sifted confectioners' sugar. Use a large, sharp knife to cut the layered pastry into rectangles measuring 2 x 4 inches. Place a second baking sheet, nonstick side down, on top of the phyllo and bake in the oven for 15 minutes. Keep hot.

Roasted apricots
Heat a griddle pan or a very large, heavy skillet. Pour in 2 tbsp olive oil and "roast" the apricot quarters, allowing them to color on both sides. Season to taste.

To serve
Place a goat's cheese, cut in half, on each plate and arrange a few quarters of roast apricot to one side. Drizzle a thin stream of the caramelized wine over the fruit. Garnish with a spicy pastry and finish with a trickle of olive oil.

Phyllo pastry is widely available now, wherever Greek or Middle-Eastern foods are sold. It should not be confused with brick/brik, another Middle-Eastern pastry, which is sold lightly cooked and is thicker. Phyllo is paper thin and very smooth. Cover the phyllo that is waiting to be used with a damp cloth as it dries out very quickly. This spicy, crunchy layered pastry is a wonderful accompaniment to the creamy texture of the fresh white goat's cheese: one of the best is Pélardon from the Cevennes, a mountainous district of south-western France.

Pan-roasted slices of water melon, soy and caramelized balsamic vinegar sauce, cream cheese shake

Soy and caramelized balsamic vinegar sauce

Mix the balsamic vinegar with the sugar in a saucepan and cook until reduced by half; add the soy sauce and set aside at room temperature.

Pan-roasted water melon slices

Cut 4 rectangular slices out of the water melon, measuring approximately 4 x 1½ inches. Dip these in the soy sauce. Melt the sugar over a moderate heat in a nonstick pan; increase the heat and 'pan-roast' the water melon slices briefly on both sides.

Cream cheese shake

Put the cheeses in a food processor or large blender; pour in the milk and olive oil. Season with salt and pepper and add the ice cubes; process at maximum speed, blending these ingredients thoroughly before pouring into chilled glasses.

To serve

Place a water melon rectangle on each plate. Surround with equal quantities of the soy and balsamic caramel sauce. Serve with the cream cheese shake.

> This very simple recipe, with its unusual preparation of the water melon, will surprise and delight your guests. The Kikkoman brand of soy sauce, with its full-bodied yet delicate flavor, is well suited to all these Far-Eastern dishes.

For the soy and caramelized balsamic vinegar sauce

¾ cup balsamic vinegar

3 tbsp superfine caster sugar

1 tbsp Kikkoman soy sauce (see note at end of method)

For the pan-roasted water melon slices

⅛ water melon

3 tbsp Kikkoman soy sauce (see note at end of method)

4 tbsp superfine sugar

For the cream cheese shake

4 small, fresh, white cow's milk cheeses

¾ cup milk, chilled

1 tbsp olive oil

salt, freshly ground white pepper

2 ice cubes

35

Vegetarian foods and vegetables

Chilled avocado smoothie with tomato and fresh chile salsa

For the avocado smoothie
4 ripe avocados
2¼ cups fresh chicken stock, chilled
juice of 1 lemon
olive oil
1 small seeded dried chile pepper, crushed
salt, freshly ground pepper

For the lemon-flavored olive oil ice cubes
3 tbsp olive oil
1 tbsp lemon juice
salt

To garnish
1 large, ripe, flavorsome tomato
small bunch cilantro
best quality sea salt freshly ground pepper
4 grissini (Italian breadsticks, see note at end of recipe)

Avocado smoothie
Peel the avocados and remove their pits. Place them in the bowl of a food processor or a blender with the chicken stock, lemon juice, a very little olive oil, and salt and pepper to taste. Process until very smooth; if the mixture is too thick, add a plain ice cube. Add as much (or as little) as you like of the crumbled dried chile (having first removed and discarded the seeds) and finish processing.

Lemon-flavored olive oil ice cubes
Beat the olive oil with the lemon juice and the salt. Fill 4 sections of an ice cube tray that has small, water-tight divisions and place in the freezer.

To serve
Peel the tomato after blanching it briefly in boiling water, remove the seeds and cut into very small dice. Take the cilantro leaves off their stalks.

Select 4 large glasses. In each of these place a small quantity of the diced tomato, followed by a few cilantro leaves. Add 1 lemon-flavored ice cube, sprinkle with coarse salt and freshly ground pepper. Place a breadstick in the glass. Serve the chilled avocado smoothie in a glass carafe and hand round, for each person to pour some into their own glass.

The creamiest avocados are the Haas type, with their rather dark, granular skins; use these if they are available. Italian *grissini* are widely sold; buy the smallest and thinnest you can find for this recipe.

Purée of artichokes, slivers of raw baby artichokes, orange popsicles, olive oil

1 lemon (to stop the
artichokes discoloring)

For the artichoke purée
14 very young violet
artichokes
2 tbsp olive oil
1 oz fat from raw, cured ham
(Bayonne, Serrano, Denhay),
very finely chopped
1 small, mild white onion or
large scallion, finely chopped
½ cup fresh chicken stock
juice of 1 lemon

**For the sliced baby
artichokes**
2 very young violet artichokes
juice of 1 lemon
scant ½ cup olive oil
1 large, ripe skinned tomato,
seeded and diced
small bunch of chives
salt, freshly ground pepper

For the orange popsicles
juice of 2 oranges
juice of ½ lemon
scant ½ cup olive oil
salt, freshly ground pepper
16 thin wooden skewers or
bamboo satay sticks

Prepare all the artichokes: 14 for the purée and 2 to be served raw.
Taking one artichoke at a time, remove the lower, outer leaves to expose the base using a very sharp, small paring knife; cut off most of the stalk, leaving only a short length of stalk attached. Cut off most of the leaves one by one, working round the artichoke and "turning" it as you do so. When done, cut off the tips of the remaining leaves. Rub all the exposed, cut surfaces with lemon juice. As each artichoke is prepared, add it to a large bowl of cold water, acidulated with lemon juice.

Orange popsicles

Place all the ingredients in a bowl and blend with a hand-held electric mixer. Season to taste. Pour into 16 watertight sections of an ice cube tray and place in the deep freeze. After 1 hour, push a wooden skewer or satay stick deep into the center of each cube and return to the freezer.

Purée of artichokes

Heat 1 tbsp olive oil with the ham fat. Cook gently for a few minutes, add the onion and continue cooking until soft but do not brown at all. Add the 14 well-drained, prepared artichoke hearts and stir for a few minutes. Sprinkle with all the chicken stock and simmer gently until the artichoke hearts are tender (approximately 20 minutes).
Place the artichokes and all their cooking juices in a food processor or blender and add the remaining olive oil and the lemon juice; process until very smooth; chill in the refrigerator.

Sliced raw artichokes

Begin by making the salsa or dressing for these: mix the lemon juice with the olive oil, tomato, chopped chives, salt, and freshly ground pepper. Use a mandoline cutter or a very sharp knife to cut the remaining 2 artichokes lengthwise into very thin slices and add to the dressing immediately to prevent them discoloring. Mix well to coat thoroughly; adjust the seasoning to taste.

To serve

Use long, narrow oval hors d'oeuvre dishes if possible: spaced out along each dish, place 4 tablespoons of the purée. Place an orange popsicle on top of each mound of purée and distribute the raw artichoke slices carefully on top, with their stalks uppermost. Garnish with the tomato salsa and more chopped chives. Serve at once.

The process of "turning" or paring the artichokes is fiddly but worth it as it reveals the most tender and intensely flavored part of the violet or "poivrade" artichoke, which flourishes in sunny climates. Always rub lemon juice immediately over cut surfaces to prevent discoloration. Fat from the best quality raw, cured ham imparts a very special flavor that adds a subtle dimension to the dish.

Tomato tartare, Moya ice cubes, toasted-almond milk

To serve 4

For the tomato tartare
4 naturally ripened, deep red, flavorsome tomatoes
bunch of chives

For the tomato granita (or ice cubes)
1¼ cups deep red tomato flesh (see note at end of method)
⅓ cup tomato juice
scant 1 tbsp thick tomato paste
1 tbsp olive oil
juice of ½ lemon
pinch of superfine sugar
salt, freshly ground pepper

For the toasted-almond milk
2 cups whole, blanched, skinned almonds
1 cup milk
1 cup crème fraîche or whole milk yogurt (see note after method on p. 116)
2 tbsp almond oil
salt, freshly ground white pepper

To serve
olive oil
small bunch of fresh basil
salt, freshly ground pepper

Preheat the oven to 360 °F.

For the tomato tartare
Blanch the tomatoes briefly in boiling water and then skin them. Remove all their seeds and cut the flesh into small dice. Set aside. Snip the chives into very short lengths and chill separately.

Tomato granita
Place the 1¼ cups of tomato flesh, cut into large pieces, into the bowl of the food processor; add the tomato juice, the tomato paste, olive oil, lemon juice, sugar, salt, and pepper. Process at very high speed, then taste and add more seasoning if necessary. Rub this purée through a strainer (a stainless-steel conical chinois if you have one) and then pour the purée into ice cube trays, with or without the divisions in place. Place in the freezer.

Toasted-almond milk
Spread the almonds out on a baking sheet and toast them in the oven for about 5–7 minutes. Take them out of the oven when they start to turn a pale golden-brown color. Bring the milk and the crème fraîche or whole milk yogurt (do not use low or nonfat yogurt) to a boil together in a large saucepan. Add the almonds, turn off the heat and leave to stand for 20 minutes to flavor the creamy milk. Add the almond oil and blend this with the almonds and milk, using a hand-held electric blender. Add salt and pepper to taste and leave to cool. Chill slightly if wished.

To serve
Season the tomato tartare with salt and pepper, add the chives.
Using individual bowls or deep soup plates, place 1 tablespoon of the tomato tartare in the bottom of each. Pour some of the chilled almond milk into each bowl. Break up the frozen tomato mixture or ice cubes with the prongs of a fork and place 1 tablespoon on top of each spoonful of tomato tartare. Add a trickle of olive oil and decorate with a sprig of basil.

> In this recipe tomatoes are given two treatments, both light and refreshing, to bring out the wonderful flavor of naturally sun-ripened tomatoes when they are in season.
> Some rare varieties (cultivated by our friend Roger Maelstaff) such as Moya, a large and very flavorsome Spanish tomato, are used in the Company des Comptoirs' restaurants.

Fruits and vegetables from other lands

Long before "fusion cooking" became fashionable, it was an everyday practice in these parts. Professor Jean-Robert Pitte's provocative dictum, "cassoulet is an American dish," springs to mind. As it happens, only the pork and duck in the recipe are native to this region, the beans and the tomatoes both coming from the New World, yet this dish epitomizes our local culinary traditions. This is no isolated phenomenon: it is a recurrent feature of all cooking. Without the ceaseless migration of ingredients and tastes facilitated by commercial contacts, chance meetings, and conquests, each country would be restricted to its own, very monotonous diet.

The great majority of the fruit and vegetables we most frequently use and enjoy originated in the natural plant nurseries of the New World and Central Asia. Sometimes we find ourselves wondering what our food would be like had the Americas never been discovered, while many of our familiar

*Above: a warehouse on the docks in the Port du Commerce in Marseilles, its windows gilded by the setting sun, evokes the thought of other sunsets, just as flamboyant, far away across the world.
Left: one of the antique maps that, together with old books about long-ago journeys and colonial prints, help create the atmosphere of travel and adventure at the Compagnie des Comptoirs.*

Below: *Zanzibar,
during the 1930s:
stenciling sacks ready
for shipping cloves.*
Right: *a band of small
bananas: this fruit
originated in India and
was introduced to the
French by the
Portuguese.*

fruits and oleaginous plants, such as almonds, apricots, peaches, cherries, walnuts, pistachios, citrus fruits, have reached Europe from Asia. Products, dishes and culinary styles migrate and, like all migrants, bring with them contributions that influence each other and intermingle. Spices, aromatics, vegetables, and fruits seem always to be on the move. Some of these imports have become so popular and widely accepted that we forget how far they have traveled from their original habitats. We assume that they have appeared on our tables since time immemorial.

Peripatetic plants

Until the early twentieth century, the orange, in common with other citrus fruits, was a rare treat and was often the only gift that children of impecunious families could expect at Christmas. Cultivated strawberries reached us only relatively recently, being brought back from Chile during the seventeenth century, although long before that the Gauls and Romans greatly enjoyed small, wild, native strawberries. The Spanish conquistadores introduced the tomato from Peru but it was

Above, left: *small, hot chiles, both green and red, are always in plentiful supply in Asian food stores.*
Above, right: *Chinese carp in one of the pools at the Compagnie des Comptoirs.*

shunned for a long time because of its sinister reputation; in common with other plants belonging to the solanaceae family it was believed to be toxic, if not devilish (tobacco, deadly nightshade, and datura are among the poisonous members). Once it was adopted by Mediterranean cooks, however, it caused so much excitement and inspired so many delicious recipes that we can only assume that it filled a culinary gap! It is one of the ironies of such migrations of foodstuffs that this native of the Andes had to wait until the nineteenth century before it was accepted in North America. Nowadays, it is as difficult to imagine Italian cooking without tomatoes as the United States without tomato ketchup! The eggplant is known to have existed four thousand years ago in East Asia, being introduced to Europe during the Middle Ages by the Muslim population of Andalusia. In the South of France, all that was missing for the invention of ratatouille was the zucchini: when marrows and sweet bell peppers arrived in their turn from the New World, this tasty selection of sun-loving vegetables was complete.

Peppers, pimentos and chiles are travelers par excellence. They have spread all over the world from Central America, where they were first discovered. In Africa and Asia, many wild and cultivated varieties have developed with the result that the capsicum has become the most varied genus of plants used for flavoring food. In Europe, the greatest quantities are consumed in Hungary (paprika) and throughout the Mediterranean basin.

A culinary laboratory

What all this tells us is that the Mediterranean region, which adopted a great number of vegetables and fruits long before they were accepted in northern countries, can be thought of as a sort of culinary laboratory through which the whole of Europe became accustomed to foods from far-off lands. The southerners' liking for strong tastes and aromas encouraged adventurous cooking, and the recipes of the Compagnie des Comptoirs perpetuate this process.

When we blend tomatoes with pineapple in a refreshing gazpacho soup or make the unexpected addition of sweet potatoes or corn to our blinis, we are being just as daring as our ancestors when they decided to add tomatoes or beans to a dish.

Tradition and innovation go hand in hand: our chilled avocado smoothie with tomato salsa and fresh chiles, for example, echoes the ingredients of Mexican guacamole. We use the sweet potato in both sweet and savory dishes, just as they do on the other side of the Atlantic. As for marrows, pumpkins, and squashes, each variety has its own distinctive taste and texture. We particularly love the small, bright orange pumpkin, the Japanese squash with its delicious chestnut taste, and the American variety, the butternut—whose name conjures up its buttery taste and consistency—as well as the muskmarrow. We serve pumpkin as a thick, creamy soup, but also use it to make sweet fritters for the dessert course.

Above: *a fruit vendor's display in a Malaysian market. Some tropical fruits are not exported to Europe and are gathered for local consumption only. The durian, with its unforgettable odor, is one example. Despite its smell, the flesh tastes good and the fruit is much sought after in Malaysia and in Hong Kong.*

Vegetarian foods and vegetables

Multicolored tomato salad made à la Roger, green tomato sorbet

For the green tomato sorbet
1–1¼ lb small green tomatoes (evergreen, see note at end of method)
½ cup sugar syrup made with ½ cup water and ½ cup sugar

For the Parmesan pastry rectangles
1 sheet of phyllo pastry
1 egg yolk
⅓ cup freshly and finely grated Parmesan cheese

For the sliced tomato salad
1 large yellow tomato
4 orange tomatoes
2 very large bright red tomatoes

To serve
pinch of superfine sugar
best sea salt (French *fleur de sel* or English Maldon if possible)
freshly grated pepper
olive oil

Green tomato sorbet

Rinse the green tomatoes and wipe them dry; cut them into large pieces and process them with the sugar syrup until the mixture is smooth. Use a sorbetière if you have one, or an ice-cream maker, to quick-freeze the mixture and then transfer to the freezer.

Parmesan pastry

Preheat the oven to 360 °F.

Cut the sheet of phyllo pastry into 4 rectangles of equal size. Brush the surface of these all over with the lightly beaten egg yolk and sprinkle evenly with freshly and finely grated Parmesan cheese. Fold the top third to the center and bottom third on top. Smooth over lightly with a rolling pin. Bake them on a baking sheet for 7–10 minutes in the oven, or until they have started to brown. Remove from the oven. Transfer to a cake rack and leave to cool.

Multicolored tomato salad

Wash the tomatoes and remove their skins; if they are very ripe these may be easy to peel off; running the blade of a knife gently, at an angle, all over the surface will help loosen the skin. If necessary blanch in boiling water for a few seconds, plunge into cold water and then peel. Remove their stalks and any hard part beneath the stalk. Slice from top to bottom into neat, thick slices.

To serve

Arrange the tomato slices, slightly overlapping, on 4 plates, alternating the colors. Sprinkle with sugar, with the special salt and with freshly ground pepper, and then drizzle a little olive oil over them.

Use a stainless-steel tablespoon to scoop out 4 egg-shaped "quenelles" of green tomato sorbet and place one in the center of each plate. Add a Parmesan pastry rectangle to each plate and serve.

Our friend Roger and the unusual varieties of tomatoes he cultivates have inspired this sensual and vividly colored version of the classic tomato salad. If you cannot get hold of these rare tomatoes, look for some unusual ones in your local stores or farmers' markets, choosing different colors (yellow, for instance) as well as differently shaped ones: Italian plum, San Marzano... Ideally, they should be home grown and fresh picked from your garden, grow-bag, or window box. When it comes to the sorbet, do not use under-ripe green tomatoes; evergreen, as the name suggests, remain green when fully ripe.

Gazpacho jelly, curried zucchini caviar, cucumber crunch

Gazpacho

Blanch, peel, trim, and seed the tomatoes. Place all the ingredients with the exception of the gelatin in the blender or food processor and process. Taste and add more seasoning if wished; strain through a fine mesh, non-metallic strainer, or stainless steel conical chinois if you have one.

You will need approximately 6 leaves of gelatin (or 1½ sachets powdered gelatin) for each 1¾ pints of gazpacho. As the quantities given for this recipe usually yield approximately 2½ pints of gazpacho, 8 or 9 leaves (2 sachets if powdered) should be enough. Soak the leaves in cold water to soften. Warm a little water gently in a pan, remove it from the heat and add the gelatin leaves. Leave them to dissolve completely, stirring occasionally. If you choose to use powdered gelatin, carrageen or agar-agar, follow the manufacturer's instructions on the packet. Add the gelling agent to the gazpacho, stirring well as you do so. Chill in the refrigerator for approximately 6 hours.

Zucchini caviar

Bring plenty of salted water to a boil in a large pan. Wash the zucchini, trim off their ends, and slice them lengthwise. Cut away or scoop out the center section, which is softer and contains the seeds, leaving only the firmer parts and the skin. Cook the strips of zucchini in the boiling water until just tender but still firm; drain and rinse well under the cold faucet. Drain in a colander; squeeze dry very gently with a clean cloth. Heat the crème fraîche or yogurt over a gentle heat, uncovered, until it has reduced and thickened considerably. Place the zucchini strips, the curry powder, olive oil, and crème

fraîche in the food processor or blender and process until very smooth. Add salt and pepper to taste. Chill in the refrigerator.

Cucumber crunch

Peel the cucumber and dice it. Add the finely snipped chives, the diced tomato, olive oil, and lemon juice; season with salt and pepper to taste.

To serve

Place 2 tablespoons of gazpacho jelly in the bottom of 4 small, deep glass dishes or coupes, cover with cucumber crunch. Spoon in the zucchini caviar and finish with a level teaspoon of plain yogurt. Sprinkle with a pinch of special salt and a twist of pepper from the peppermill. Trickle a little olive oil on top, followed by a pinch of curry powder.

> We make this recipe with our favorite tomato grower's produce, but you can substitute any other varieties, provided they are really ripe, full flavored, and fragrant. If you want to embellish the dish further, cut slivers of young zucchini and deep-fry these until crisp; use them to decorate this refreshing appetizer: the crispiness will complement the summery vegetables.

To serve 4

Gazpacho jelly
2½–2¾ lb ripe, deep red tomatoes
3¼ cups tomato juice
1 tsp tomato paste
scant ½ cup olive oil
pinch of superfine sugar
juice of 1 lemon
salt, freshly ground pepper
8 or 9 leaves of gelatin (see method for alternatives)

For the zucchini caviar
6 medium-sized zucchini
scant ½ cup crème fraîche or whole milk yogurt (see note after method on p. 116)
generous pinch of mild or medium curry powder
3 tbsp olive oil
salt, freshly ground pepper

For the cucumber crunch
1 cucumber
small bunch of chives
1 very red, ripe tomato (see recipe on p. 48), seeded, diced
1 tbsp olive oil
a squeeze of lemon juice
salt, freshly ground pepper

To serve
1 small pot plain, whole milk yoghurt
olive oil
mild or medium curry powder
best quality sea salt, freshly ground pepper

vegetarian first courses

Fried vine tomatoes, mozzarella, lettuce heart, balsamic caramel dressing

To serve 4

4 bunches or sprays of cherry
vine tomatoes (approximately
12 tomatoes on each)
1¼ cups balsamic vinegar
juice of 1 lemon
olive oil
salt, freshly ground pepper

To serve

1 or 2 very fresh, large, pale-
green lettuce hearts
9 oz buffalo milk
mozzarella cheese(s)
fresh chervil for decoration
olive oil
best sea salt (English
Maldon, French *fleur de sel*)

Heat the balsamic vinegar and cook, uncovered, over a gentle heat until it acquires a syrupy consistency. Check by tilting the pan to one side: if the syrup leaves a light coating on the bottom of the pan, it is ready. Watch carefully during the later stages of the reduction as it can burn easily! Rinse the lettuce leaves and dry with paper towels. Make a vinaigrette with the lemon juice, 2 tablespoons olive oil, salt, and pepper. Heat a little olive oil in a skillet, place the sprays of tomatoes in the pan and cook over a gentle heat.

To serve

Slice the mozzarella cheese(s) thickly and arrange on 4 plates, adding the lettuce leaves tossed in the lemon vinaigrette and one spray of vine tomatoes per portion. Sprinkle with a little olive oil, the balsamic caramel dressing, and some special sea salt. Decorate with sprigs of chervil.

A delicious cocktail of Italian tastes, subtly enhanced by the caramelized balsamic vinegar. The best lettuce to use for this recipe is the butterhead.

Quick tomato and pineapple gazpacho, lime and soy granita

To serve 4

For the lime and soy granita
¾ cup superfine sugar
scant ½ cup light soy sauce
juice of 3 limes
scant ½ cup water

For the tomato and pineapple gazpacho
2¼ lb deep red, ripe tomatoes
1 small ripe pineapple
pinch of caster sugar
scant ½ cup olive oil
salt, freshly ground pepper

To serve
1 ripe, very red tomato
(see preparation method
on p. 48), seeded
small bunch chives
olive oil

Lime and soy granita

The day before you plan to serve this dish, make a syrup with the sugar and 1 cup water. Mix the soy sauce, lime juice, and the extra water with the finished, cooled syrup in a freezer-proof, nonmetallic or plastic bowl and place in the freezer for at least 12 hours.

Tomato and pineapple gazpacho

Blanch and skin the tomatoes; cut them into large pieces, discarding the seeds and any tough parts. Peel the pineapple, remove the hard central section, and cut the flesh into cubes. Place the tomatoes, three-quarters of the pineapple flesh, a pinch of sugar, and the olive oil in the bowl of a food processor and reduce to a smooth purée. Season with salt and pepper to taste. Chill in the refrigerator.

To serve

Cut the remaining pineapple flesh and the tomato into very small dice. Mix with the finely snipped or chopped chives. Chill in the refrigerator.

Using deep soup plates or shallow bowls, place 1–2 tablespoons of the chilled tomato, pineapple, and chive mixture in each. Use the prongs of a fork to break up the lemon-soy sorbet and shape the resulting granita into 4 oval "quenelles" using 2 tablespoons; place each one, as soon as it has been shaped, on top of the tomato, pineapple, and chive mixture. Surround with the chilled gazpacho and finish with a trickle of olive oil.

> You have probably never tried the combination of tomato and pineapple: you will enjoy this harmonious blend of summer tastes, a mixture of aromatic sweetness, freshness, and sharpness. Every component of this recipe must be served while still very cold.

Pasta with broccoli, arugula pesto, and grilled Provolone cheese

Arugula pesto

Put the arugula, the peeled garlic cloves, and the olive oil in the food processor; add a little salt and then process to a smooth paste. Mix thoroughly in a bowl with the ground almonds, the Parmesan cheese, and pepper to taste.

Orecchiette pasta and broccoli

Trim and wash the broccoli; detach the floret tops and set aside. Use the upper part of the stalk and the beginnings of the "branches" from which you have cut the florets and cut into slivers with a mandoline or a very sharp knife.

Boil the broccoli florets in plenty of salted water for only a few minutes, until they are barely tender. Rinse them immediately under the cold faucet, drain and set aside.

Bring to a boil plenty of salted water with a few drops of olive oil added to it in a large pan. Add the pasta and cook until al dente (tender but still with a little "bite" to it); drain at once. Heat 1 tablespoon olive oil in a nonstick skillet and fry the thinly sliced pieces of broccoli stalks briefly over a moderate heat until just tender. Season to taste.

To serve

Mix the florets and the stalks gently together, off the heat. Add to the hot pasta, with 3 tablespoons of the arugula pesto, the crème fraîche or yogurt, and diced tomato. Slice the Provolone cheese; heat briefly over a high heat, turning once, in the nonstick skillet, place on top of the pasta and broccoli, and serve immediately.

This Italian-inspired dish can be served either as a first course or as a light main course. Be careful not to overcook the florets: they should be tender but firm, as should the stalks. For a stronger taste, use unmatured Pecorino, a sheep's milk cheese with the same semihard consistency as Provolone when it has not been allowed to age. Provolone, a pressed curd cow's milk cheese, varies from mild to fairly full flavored, depending on maturation. Use the best, fruitiest olive oil.

To serve 4

For the arugula pesto
3½ oz arugula leaves, washed and dried
5 cloves of garlic, peeled
2 cups olive oil
⅔ cup ground almonds
½ cup freshly grated Parmesan cheese
salt, freshly ground pepper

For the pasta and broccoli
1¾ cups orecchiette or similar fresh short pasta
5 oz broccoli head
olive oil
salt, freshly ground pepper

To serve
1 tbsp crème fraîche or whole milk yogurt
1 skinned tomato (see recipe on p. 48), seeded and diced
5 oz Provolone Italian cheese (see note at end of method)

53

Baby violet artichokes Italian-style, arugula salad, Parmesan shavings

For the tomates confites
3 ripe, deep red tomatoes
2 cups olive oil
2 pinches of superfine sugar
2 pinches of salt

For the caramelized balsamic vinegar
2 cups balsamic vinegar

For the marinated artichokes
12 baby violet artichokes
2 lemons (to prevent discoloration of the artichokes)
2 cups olive oil
scant ½ cup white wine vinegar

For the basil-flavoured oil
1 large bunch fresh basil
1 cup olive oil
salt

For the arugula salad
4 oz arugula leaves
3 tbsp olive oil
1 tbsp lemon juice
salt, freshly ground pepper

Garnish with
8 Parmesan cheese shavings

Slow-baked tomatoes (tomates confites)

Preheat the oven to 175 °F.
Make small surface slits in the tomato skins and plunge them into boiling water for 10–20 seconds (depending on how ripe they are). Immediately transfer them to a bowl of iced water (use ice cubes). Peel and quarter them, remove the inner divisions, the seeds and any hard parts, leaving just quarters or "petals" of flesh. Cover a baking sheet with non-stick wax or silicone paper; sprinkle the surface with half the olive oil and half the sugar and salt. Spread out the tomato petals in a single layer. Sprinkle with the remaining sugar, salt, and oil. Slow bake the tomatoes in the oven (this method extracts a considerable amount of their moisture) for approximately 2½ hours, turning them from time to time.

Caramelized balsamic vinegar

Pour the vinegar into a pan and reduce over a low heat until it thickens into a syrup. Take care not to let it burn! It is ready when the syrup leaves a thin coating on the bottom of the pan when the pan is tilted to one side. Set aside.

Marinated artichokes

Trim or "turn" the artichokes (see recipe on page 38 for method of preparation). When they are all done, drain off the acidulated water, blot dry and roast on a ribbed griddle or ridged dry-skillet over a high heat, turning once: they are meant to show sear lines. Transfer the artichokes to a casserole dish and add sufficient oil and vinegar to cover them. Cook over a very low heat until the artichokes are tender but still crisp. Leave in the liquid to cool completely before serving.

Basil-flavored oil

Place the basil leaves, removed from their stalks, in a food processor or blender, add a pinch of salt and the olive oil. Process at high speed. (This oil will keep for several days in a cool place or larder fridge.)

Arugula salad

Dress the prepared arugula with the mixture of olive oil, lemon juice, salt, and pepper.

To serve

Remove the artichokes from the marinade, draining them well; arrange 3 on each plate and place the arugula salad in the center of the plate. Surround with a ribbon of basil-flavored oil and another of caramelized balsamic vinegar. Garnish each serving with 3 tomato "petals" and two Parmesan cheese shavings.

> These marinated artichokes keep well in the refrigerator, covered in olive oil, until you need them and can be used in other salads as an interesting extra ingredient. You can preserve the "petals" of slow-baked tomato (tomates confites) in the same way.

Griddle-roasted pumpkin, pumpkin soup, ricotta dumplings

For the griddle-roasted pumpkin

1 small, whole orange-fleshed pumpkin

olive oil

best quality sea salt (*fleur de sel*, Maldon)

For the cream of pumpkin hot soup drink

1 lb 2 oz pumpkin (or butternut squash)

1 mild white onion

½ stick/2 oz unsalted butter

pinch of superfine sugar

1¾ pints chicken stock

3¾ oz peeled, cooked, unsweetened vacuum-packed sweet chestnuts

½ cup light (pouring) cream

salt, freshly ground pepper

For the ricotta dumplings

½ cup very fresh ricotta cheese

1 cup coarsely crushed unsalted pistachio nuts

1 tbsp coarsely crushed pine nuts (kernels)

1 tbsp golden raisins, coarsely chopped

juice of ½ lemon

olive oil

salt, freshly ground pepper

Wash the small, whole pumpkin and cut it into neat, fairly thin sections (see facing page); discard the seeds and filaments; do not peel the slices.

Blanch for 4 minutes in boiling water; drain and set aside.

Cream of pumpkin hot soup drink

Peel the generous 1 lb piece of pumpkin or squash and remove the seeds and filaments. Dice the flesh. Peel and cut the onion into very thin slices and cook these over a gentle heat in the butter until tender but do not allow to color. Add the diced pumpkin flesh, the sugar, chicken stock, and the chestnuts (these unsweetened cooked chestnuts are available in tins or plastic vacuum packs in many good food stores); bring to the boil and simmer until the diced pumpkin is tender. When it is cooked, add the cream, bring back to a boil; remove from the heat immediately. Blend or process until smooth; season to taste and keep hot.

Ricotta cheese dumplings

Mix all the ingredients together, beating well to incorporate plenty of air.

Griddle-roasted pumpkin

Cook the pumpkin slices on a lightly oiled griddle (or use a very large, heavy skillet) until tender, allowing them to brown well on both sides; sprinkle with best quality sea salt.

To serve

Place 2 or 3 slices of roasted pumpkin in the center of 4 individual plates; shape the ricotta mixture into 4 oval dumplings (see facing page) using 2 tablespoons, and place each one across the center of the pumpkin slices; surround with a trickle of oil. Serve the cream of pumpkin soup very hot, in preheated glasses, and sprinkle a few drops of the best quality olive oil on the top of each serving.

Pumpkin is a member of the squash family and this variety originates from Japan; it is popular for its vivid orange flesh and has a taste reminiscent of sweet chestnuts. Butternut squash resembles it in taste and texture. Both go extremely well with chestnuts and dried vine fruits.

Corn blinis, baby spinach, prosciutto

**For the slow-baked
tomatoes**
2 very red tomatoes
3½ tbsp olive oil
2 pinches of salt
2 pinches of superfine sugar

For the vinaigrette
juice of 1 lemon
5 tbsp olive oil
salt, freshly ground pepper

For the corn blinis
½ cup canned corn kernels
1 scant cup all-purpose flour
2 eggs
1 level tbsp baking powder
¾ cup milk
pinch of salt
leaves from a small bunch of
fresh cilantro, chopped
a little olive oil

To serve
1 packet baby spinach
(select 60 leaves)
4 large, thin slices of
prosciutto (see note at end
of method)

Slow-baked tomatoes

Preheat the oven to 175 °F.

Make small slits in the skin of the tomatoes
and place in boiling water for 20 seconds.
Transfer them without delay to a bowl of iced
water, then peel and quarter them, removing
the seeds and the inner divisions, leaving just
the outer flesh "petals." Cover a baking sheet
with nonstick wax or silicone paper, sprinkle it
with half the oil, followed by half the salt and
sugar. Spread out the tomato quarters, well
spaced out in a single layer and sprinkle with
the remaining sugar and salt, followed by the
remaining olive oil. Bake the tomatoes in the
oven for approximately 2½ hours, turning them
from time to time.

The vinaigrette

Mix all the ingredients and season with salt and
pepper to taste.

Corn blinis

Make the batter: mix all the ingredients well
(with the exception of the olive oil and the
cilantro); the mixture should be thicker than
conventional pancake batter. Add the chopped
cilantro leaves and season to taste. Heat the
olive oil in a wide, nonstick skillet. Add the
batter, a tablespoon at a time, and cook in the
same way as drop-scones, turning once. Cook
another batch of 4, so you have 2 blinis per
person.

To serve

Have the baby spinach leaves ready rinsed
and dried; toss them briefly in the lemon
vinaigrette.

Place one blini on each plate, place a slice
of *prosciutto* on this, followed by 2 tomato
"petals." Add some baby spinach salad and
top with a blini.

> Parma or San Daniele is the best
> quality cured Italian ham (prosciutto)
> and it must be thinly sliced. The use of
> the corn in the blinis adds a pleasing
> sweetness and agreeable texture.

Marinated salmon and breadsticks, artichoke hearts "barigoule" with turmeric

To serve 4

For the spiced salmon
9 oz salmon fillet
½ cup sea salt
1 tbsp muscovado soft
brown sugar
pinch of finely crushed
black peppercorns
small bunch fresh dill
leaves, chopped
12 very small, thin Italian
breadsticks (*grissini*)

For the artichokes
12 baby violet artichokes
juice of 1 lemon
1 lemon, cut in half
2 tbsp olive oil
1 large scallion
scant ½ cup dry white wine
1 garlic clove, crushed
1 bay leaf
sprig of thyme
2 inches fresh turmeric root,
grated (see note)
salt, freshly ground pepper

**Dressing for the
artichokes "barigoule"**
juice of ½ lemon
a few fresh cilantro leaves
1 prepared ripe, red tomato
(see p. 48), chopped
2 tbsp extra-virgin olive oil
salt, freshly ground pepper

To serve
scant ½ cup mascarpone
fresh cilantro
salt, freshly ground pepper

Begin by preparing the salmon: mix the salt with the sugar and pepper and rub well into the salmon fillet; add the finely snipped dill. Place a small board and a weight on top of the fish and chill for 6 hours in the refrigerator.

Artichokes à la barigoule

Prepare the artichokes, using a small, very sharp knife: leave 1–1¼ inch of the stalk attached, remove the lowest, outermost leaves and then snip off the top halves of the remaining leaves, working your way from the stalk toward the innermost leaves, leaving only the heart of the artichoke. Make sure that you end up with what looks like a bud. Cut off the tips of the innermost leaves and scoop out the "choke" with a sharp-edged teaspoon. As you trim away parts of each artichoke, rub the cut surfaces with the lemon half; add each artichoke to a bowl of cold water acidulated with lemon juice to prevent discolouration. Heat the olive oil in a deep pan and cook the finely chopped scallion without browning it. Add the well-drained artichokes, cut lengthwise into quarters, then the white wine, followed by the garlic, bay leaf, thyme, and turmeric. Bring to a boil, adding enough water to cover the artichokes. Simmer until the artichokes are tender but still crisp, seasoning with salt and pepper. When they are done, take them out of the pan and reduce the cooking liquid by boiling, uncovered. Return the artichokes to the liquid and leave to cool.

Marinated salmon

Shortly before it is time to serve the salmon, rinse the fillet under the cold faucet and blot dry with paper towels. Use a ham-cutting knife or similar very sharp knife to cut 12 very thin horizontal slices from the salmon fillet. Wind each of them around a breadstick.

Dressing for the artichokes

Drain the artichokes through a fine-mesh strainer. Collect the liquid in a bowl and mix in the lemon, cilantro leaves, chopped tomato and olive oil. Season to taste.

To serve

Mix a little salt and pepper with the mascarpone, beating briefly with a fork.
In each of 4 deep glass coupes or small bowls, place 12 artichoke quarters, sprinkle with the dressing. Use a dessert spoon to scoop out an egg-shaped "dumpling" of mascarpone and place on top of the artichokes. Finally, top each serving with 3 salmon-wrapped breadsticks. Garnish with sprigs of cilantro.

This recipe draws on the cooking of three parts of the world for its inspiration: the artichoke dish comes from the Mediterranean hinterland of France; turmeric and cilantro from south-east Asia and the marinated salmon from Scandinavia. Asian greengrocers sell fresh turmeric, a slender rhizome reminiscent of fresh ginger in appearance but with bright orange flesh and orangey-gray skin. You can use 1 level dessertspoon of ground turmeric instead.

Duck brochettes, eggy-bread and giblet croutons, mixed baby-leaf salad

3 duck breasts
(or 6 *aiguillettes*, see method)
12 bamboo skewers or
satay sticks
olive oil
salt, freshly ground pepper

**For the eggy-bread and
giblet paté croutons**
3 tbsp port wine
1 shallot, finely chopped
3 duck livers
2 duck hearts
1¼ cups milk
1 large egg, lightly beaten
4 French bread slices
(baguette loaf), cut on the
slant
olive oil
salt, freshly ground pepper

**For the mixed baby-leaf
salad**
1 large packet mixed baby
salad leaves
3 tbsp hazelnut oil
1 tbsp sherry vinegar
salt, freshly ground pepper

Aiguillettes are long, thick slices of breast meat taken from either side of the breast bone; if you use these, cut each one in half lengthwise. If using duck breasts, slice each one lengthwise into 4 thick strips and thread them onto bamboo skewers.

Place the port wine and the chopped shallot in a pan and reduce until there is hardly any liquid left. Set aside.

Place the washed, trimmed duck livers and hearts in the food processor and process. Add the reduced port wine and shallot, and a little salt and pepper; process very briefly. Transfer this mixture to a bowl and chill in the refrigerator.

Mixed baby-leaf salad

Make a vinaigrette with the hazelnut oil and sherry vinegar; season with salt and pepper. Set aside.

Eggy-bread and giblet croutons

Pour the milk into a shallow dish and beat the egg lightly in a separate dish. Spread an even amount of the giblet mixture firmly onto each bread slice to make it adhere. Dip each slice first in the milk, allow it to absorb the milk, and then dip briefly in the beaten egg.

Heat a very little olive oil in a wide, nonstick skillet; add the eggy-bread, giblet spread side down. Allow to fry and brown for 3–4 minutes, then turn over and brown the other side.

Cooking the duck brochettes

Pan-fry the skewered duck strips in the same wide, nonstick skillet adding a very little more olive oil if necessary. Turn them once; the flesh should be brown on the outside but pink on the inside. Season with salt and pepper.

To serve

Toss the salad in the prepared vinaigrette. Place 3 duck brochettes on each plate, together with an eggy-bread and giblet crouton and some mixed baby-leaf salad. Serve at once, while the crouton and duck are still hot.

> This unpretentious, rather rustic dish is an echo of long-ago duck shoots in the Languedoc and Cévennes areas of France, when feathered game used to be served accompanied by its giblets on slices of bread. Hazelnut oil adds an autumnal note.

Hot onion tart with tomatoes, sardines, and herb salad

To serve 4

2¼ lb freshly caught sardines, filleted, trimmed
4 deep red, ripe tomatoes
2 oz piece Parmesan cheese
4 rounds, 4 inches wide, cut out of a sheet of puff pastry
salt, freshly ground pepper

For the onion compote
7 medium-sized, mild white onions, very thinly sliced
1½ tbsp butter
pinch of superfine sugar
salt, freshly ground pepper

For the lemon and honey vinaigrette
juice of 3 lemons
2 tbsp clear, runny honey
1 cup olive oil
salt, freshly ground pepper

For the herb salad
a few arugula leaves
small bunch of chives, snipped into fairly long lengths
leaves from a small bunch of very fresh cilantro
leaves from a small bunch of chervil

Use paper towels to blot the sardine fillets dry, wiping off any remaining scales. Make sure all visible bones have been removed. Blanch the tomatoes for a few seconds in boiling water and peel them. Use a cheese slicer or potato peeler to shave off flakes of Parmesan. Set all this aside ready for use.

Preheat the oven to 425 °F.

Onion compote

Cook the onions in the butter until tender without allowing them to color. Add the pinch of sugar. Cover and cook over a very low heat for 20 minutes or until very soft indeed, then remove the lid and allow any excess moisture to reduce and evaporate. Season to taste and keep hot.

Lemon and honey vinaigrette

Mix all the ingredients listed for this dressing.

Preparation and cooking of the pastry base

Use ready-made puff pastry; roll out to a thin sheet and cut out 4 rounds measuring 4 inches across; transfer these onto a nonstick baking sheet. Prick all over the exposed surfaces with the prongs of a fork to prevent them rising too much as they cook and, for the same reason, place another baking sheet, nonstick side down, on top of the rounds. Bake in the oven for 15 minutes. When they are done, take them out of the oven and turn up the oven temperature to 475 °F.

Spread a generous tablespoonful of onion compote on each pastry round (you will need to reserve a small amount for assembling this dish); slice the tomatoes fairly thickly and arrange on top of the onions. Add the sardine fillets; season with salt and pepper. Top with the Parmesan shavings. Place in the hot oven for a few minutes to lightly cook the sardines and soften the cheese slightly.

To serve

While the pastries are in the oven, dress the herb salad with some of the lemon and honey vinaigrette.

Spread one-quarter of the remaining onion compote in the center of each plate and put a pastry round on top of it (this will stop them sliding around); garnish each tart with some of the salad. Encircle with a trace of olive oil and serve at once.

A traditional recipe from Nice, *pissaladière niçoise*, inspired us to include onions cooked in this way when creating these savory pastries. White onions are chosen for the delicious sweet taste they develop after long, slow cooking. Return to the very hot oven for only as long as it takes to part-cook the sardines: they are so fresh all they need is to heat through and become firmer.

Home-smoked mackerel fillets, sweet potato blinis, chive-flavored oil

To serve 4

For the smoked mackerel fillets
2 medium-sized very fresh mackerel
1 tbsp beech wood sawdust (see note at end of method)
best sea salt, freshly ground pepper

For the chive-flavoured oil
1 bunch chives
scant ½ cup olive oil
salt

For the blinis
7 oz sweet potatoes (orange flesh variety)
scant ½ cup all-purpose flour
1 egg
3–4 tsp plain whole-milk yogurt
olive oil
salt, freshly ground pepper

Fillet the mackerel, using tweezers to remove any remaining bones. Set aside.

Chive-flavored oil

Put the oil, a generous pinch of salt and the rinsed, dried chives into the blender. Process until completely blended; set aside.

Blinis

Cook the sweet potatoes in plenty of boiling water. When they are very tender, peel them. Mash to a fine purée and, when lukewarm, mix in the flour and egg and season with salt and pepper. Add a little yogurt at a time to achieve a thick pancake batter consistency. Heat a lightly oiled, nonstick skillet and, when hot, add spoonfuls of the batter, sufficient to make only very small pancakes or mini-blinis. Brown lightly on both sides and allow 2–3 per person.

Home-smoked mackerel fillets

Sprinkle 1 tbsp of the beech sawdust into a very wide, nonstick skillet. Place a rack on top of this to prevent the fish coming into direct contact with the beech wood shavings; arrange the fish fillets on the rack. Cover tightly and cook over a high heat for approximately 5 minutes (the smoking time will vary, depending on the thickness of the fillets).

To serve

Make an attractive arrangement on each plate, with the blinis on one side and the smoked fish in the middle, surrounded by a thin ribbon of chive dressing. Sprinkle the fish with a little Maldon or *fleur de sel* best quality sea salt and with a little freshly milled pepper.

You will find smoking fish at home much easier following this method than you ever imagined. The fish must not touch the wood shavings and should rest on a rack or raised, slotted aluminum disk. Sawdust for smoking can be obtained from a smokery supplier or a reputable small-scale sawmill; fruitwood (e.g. apple wood) can also be used.

Raw bream salad, bread "crumble," grated lemon zest dressing

To serve 4

For the crumble

1 large, oven-baked (i.e. not steam-baked) white loaf to yield 4½ cups (topped down) breadcrumbs

2¼ sticks/9 oz butter, softened at room temperature

2 cups all-purpose flour

salt

For the raw bream salad

1 lb absolutely fresh fillets of gilthead bream with its skin intact but scales removed

olive oil

3 blanched and skinned tomatoes (see recipe on p. 56), finely diced

1 bunch chives

small bunch fresh cilantro

juice of 2 lemons

salt, freshly ground pepper

To serve

1 small tub plain yogurt

finely grated zest of 1 untreated, unsprayed lemon

best quality sea salt

freshly ground pepper

Bread "crumble"

Cut off all the crusts from the bread; cut the loaf into thick slices and spread out on the racks of the oven, preheated to 195 °F to bake very gently for approximately 1 hour or until dry and pale golden brown. Place in the food processor and process to fine breadcrumbs. Turn up the oven temperature to 340 °F. Using the tips of your fingers or a utensil (a pastry blender), combine the butter (softened at room temperature) with the flour until it has the classic "crumble" consistency for making a crisp topping (British crumble topping). Add the breadcrumbs and a little salt; mix briefly together. Place very small mounds of this mixture, pinched into shape to make them hold firm, spaced out on a baking sheet and bake in the oven for 10 minutes or until pale golden brown. Set aside in a warm, dry place.

Raw bream salad

Remove the skin from the bream fillets. Cover a baking sheet with a sheet of wax paper, lightly brush the surface with olive oil, and spread the skin out on it. Cover with another sheet of lightly oiled wax paper and then place another baking sheet on top. Cook in a preheated oven at 325 °F for about 15–20 minutes, or until the skin is dry and crunchy. Alternatively, cook the bream skin in a nonstick skillet with a very little olive oil over a gentle heat until crisp, but the skin must still be kept flat: cover with oiled wax paper (oiled side against the fish skin) and place the bottom of a heavy pan that fits neatly into the skillet on top of the paper. Check the skin from time to time; this second method should take no longer than 15 minutes; when it is crisp and crunchy, leave to cool and then set aside, uncovered, in a warm, dry place.

Dice the bream fillets. Marinate them for 5 minutes in a bowl of salted water. Snip or chop the chives finely and take the cilantro leaves off their stalks. Set both aside. Drain the diced fish very thoroughly; mix it with the diced tomato, lemon juice, chives, cilantro leaves and ⅓–½ cup olive oil. Add extra seasoning to taste.

To serve

Use small, fairly deep dishes or Japanese bowls in which to serve this first course: place a generous tablespoonful of diced fish salad in each dish and sprinkle with a layer of the "crumble." On top of the "crumble," drizzle a scant teaspoonful of yogurt. Decorate with a pinch of finely grated lemon zest, sprinkle with a little freshly ground pepper and a pinch of sea salt (*fleur de sel* or Maldon) and then garnish with a piece of the crisped skin.

You can cut down on preparation time by using good quality (not artificially colored) commercially prepared breadcrumbs. Use only the very freshest fish; do not use farmed bream; gilthead bream is one of the best but you can also use sea bream, porgy, or any true member of the bream family. You can use fresh lime juice and zest instead of lemon.

Western Mediterranean

It is hardly surprising that our cooking bears a recognizably regional imprint, since this is the environment, in its widest sense, in which we have been immersed from childhood. Spain, southern France, Italy, and their islands make up the western Mediterranean. Languedoc is thought of as looking toward Spain, while Provence appears more drawn toward Italy, but each of these two regions has its own, unique character, with their respective frontiers being bounded by narrow stretches of land that also possess their own strong personalities. Roussillon is the conduit through which Catalonia's influence reaches France. Even the Comté of Nice, despite its proximity, is more Genoese than Provençal in character: here, the focus is on green vegetables, ravioli, and pesto made with fresh herbs in much the same way as in Genoa and in Savona. At the heart of this region lies the Camargue: peaceful, inscrutable, watching over its wild white horses and herds of cattle.

Above: *displays of papayas and oranges in a market in Madeira.* Left: *a truly Latin combination of colors and atmosphere in the bar at the Compagnie des Comptoirs in Montpellier.*

Montpellier is very close to the Camargue, at the centre of Midi tradition and culture. Thus placed, we realize how much these differing areas have in common.

A certain way of life

Here we find squares shaded by large plane trees and people indulging in endless, desultory conversation over glasses of *anis del Mono, pastis,* or *anisette*. Nibbling *tapas* in Spain, or *antipasti* in Italy, is the western way of observing the ritual of "little dishes" so beloved throughout the Mediterranean basin. A siesta is taken during the early afternoon, the better to enjoy oneself—or do business—in the evening. Stores stay open till late. The streets teem with life, especially after nightfall; cool gardens hide behind sturdy walls; and pots of basil flourish on window sills for all to admire. The air of nonchalance is more apparent than real: the sun may sap people's physical energy, but not their wits. On the waterfront, sea urchins, or violets, are consumed with chilled white wine to the sound of the lapping sea. Fish are grilled in the open air over fires of vine prunings lit between stones. Wine-producing villages are redolent of grape *marc* and the scent of *belles-de-nuit*, those fragrant jalapa flowers that bloom at night. The shared treasures of this world are olive oil, almonds, vines, honey, anchovies, tuna, tomatoes, candied fruits, and rich, syrupy wines oxidized to a carefully calculated degree; the patisseries are full of the scent of orange peel in Spain and bitter almonds in Italy. Tomatoes, figs, grapes, and pears are savored with fresh, white cheeses: ricotta, brocciu (from Corsica), brousse niçoise (ewe's milk cheese), mozzarella, mild Provolone. The stronger, harder cheeses such as Parmesan and pecorino accompany pasta dishes; Spanish manchego cheese is enjoyed as a *tapa*, with slices of *membrillo* (pieces of quince jelly).

Our gastronomic points of reference

In our cooking, acknowledgements of our debt to Spain and Italy recur constantly, like affectionate winks of recognition. From Spain we have adopted Iberian raw, cured ham, amazingly tender and sweet—even the fat is a delicacy. We make gazpacho with jellied tomato juice or with pineapple flesh, since it is essential to maintain the freshness and lightness of this first course inspired by the Andalusian sun. We have also adopted a Spanish cooking technique, that of grilling *à la plancha* on a griddle with shallow ridges, the ideal way to sear and seal in all the flavor of meats, fish, crustaceans, vegetables, and even fruits. We use this method too to grill asparagus and *parillada* steak, the juicy and flavorsome rib-of-beef cut that is only to be found at its best between the Camargue and Gibraltar. We also cook one of our signature dishes *à la plancha*: squid with lemon confit, an enduring favorite on our menu.

Travelling east, toward Italy, we reinterpret the classic dishes of the coast of Languedoc and Provence. Hot onion tart is our version of Nice's *pissaladière*; garnished with fresh tomato and virtually raw sardines that are given the briefest cooking, a mere heating through in a very hot oven. Our mixed vegetable tart is enhanced by *pistou*, the Italo-Niçoise sauce that we also prepare with arugula leaves, an archetypal Italian salad herb if ever there was one. The little *poivrades* or violet artichokes that have such an intense flavor are served as an antipasto or as a freshly prepared purée accompanied by slices of raw baby artichokes. We also pay tribute to the cheeses that come from the other side of the Alps: ricotta beaten to a frothy lightness with dried vine fruits, grilled Provolone, mozzarella served with roast tomatoes, Parmesan shavings scattered over salads. And, of course, pasta—without which there could be no authentic Mediterranean cuisine—but we reserve the right to translate lasagne into our own dialect by introducing layers of fresh vegetables that have been stir-fried in a wok… and beckons us much farther toward the east.

Above: *the sea urchin, a little invertebrate that protects itself with its spines; deep inside are the orange gonads or coral, tasting delicately of iodine and of the sea, that are savored throughout the Mediterranean area.*

Chilled mousseline of sweet potato, langoustines and seafood aspic with crème fraîche topping

For the langoustines
(Dublin Bay prawns)

12 large langoustines

2 tbsp olive oil

1 carrot, diced

1 medium-sized onion, diced

1 leek, diced

1 celery stalk, diced

1 tomato, peeled, seeded,
and chopped

1 bouquet garni

2 egg whites

½–¾ cup extra langoustine
flesh (or white fish)

1 small onion, thinly sliced

1 leek, sliced into thin rounds

1 carrot, sliced into thin rounds

6 gelatin leaves

salt, ground white pepper

Mousseline of
sweet potato

4 sweet potatoes (orange flesh)

2 tbsp crème fraîche or
whipping cream, stiffly beaten

a pinch of superfine sugar

salt, ground white pepper

For the artichoke salad

2 young violet artichokes

juice of 1 lemon

3 tbsp olive oil

1 tomato

small bunch of chives, snipped

salt, freshly ground white
pepper

To garnish

scant ½ cup crème fraîche or
whipping cream, stiffly beaten

a few drops of lemon juice

freshly ground white pepper

Langoustines and seafood aspic

Take the heads off the langoustines before peeling them; keep the heads and shells. Slit down the back of the langoustines with the tip of a small, sharp knife and remove the dark-colored intestinal tract.

Fry the langoustines' heads and shells gently in the olive oil in a pan; add the cleaned, diced vegetables, the chopped tomato, and the bouquet garni. Continue frying gently while stirring for a few minutes, then add sufficient water to cover the contents of the pan completely. Bring slowly to a boil, cover, and simmer for approximately 30 minutes. Leave to cool, then strain through a fine strainer.

Return this fish stock to the cleaned pan, add the peeled langoustines and poach them for 2 minutes; remove them from the stock, rinse very briefly in cold water, and set aside. Clarify the stock: place the egg whites, the ½–¾ cup extra langoustine flesh or white filleted fish and the second batch of prepared, thinly sliced vegetables in a food processor; process until very smoothly blended. Add this mixture to the fish stock, bring to a boil and simmer for 20 minutes over a low heat, stirring gently during the first few minutes.

Gently pour the stock through a fine mesh, conical (chinois) strainer; add seasoning to taste. Measure out 1¾ pints of the hot stock and add the softened gelatin leaves. Leave to stand away from the heat and when the gelatin has completely dissolved, pour the clarified stock into a stainless steel or glass bowl and chill in the refrigerator.

Cooking the sweet potatoes

Boil the unpeeled sweet potatoes for approximately 30 minutes. Drain thoroughly, peel, and purée. Season with salt and pepper, transfer to a bowl, and chill in the refrigerator.

Artichoke salad

Trim the artichokes (see recipe on page 44), placing them in a bowl of cold water acidulated with lemon juice to prevent discoloration. Dice the artichokes finely and sprinkle with lemon juice. Add the olive oil, salt, and pepper and mix thoroughly. Add the peeled, seeded, and diced tomato and the snipped chives.

Mousseline of sweet potato

Stir the 2 tablespoons of stiffly beaten crème fraîche into the puréed sweet potato. Season to taste, adding the sugar if necessary.

To serve

Beat the remaining crème fraîche with a few drops of lemon juice.

Serve in glass coupes or bowls: place 2 tablespoons of sweet potato in each bowl, cover with a layer of diced artichoke salad and place 3 chilled langoustines on top of each serving. Add the langoustine aspic and top with 1 teaspoon of acidulated crème fraiche. Grind a little pepper on top and serve chilled.

> This is an appetizer for a special occasion. Make sure you use very fresh raw langoustines or the best deep frozen ones available. Langoustines are often marketed as Dublin Bay prawns or Norway lobsterettes. For a real treat, add 1 scant teaspoon of Sevruga caviar to each serving, placed on top of the dab of lemon-flavored crème fraîche.

Langoustines with thyme flowers, baby fennel and radish salad, horseradish vinaigrette

Having removed the crustaceans' heads, use small, pointed scissors to snip down the back of each langoustine, stopping just short of the tail flippers. Remove the shell and extract the black or dark gray intestinal tract; leave the tail flippers attached, intact (see note at end of method). Slice the red onion very finely, place in a bowl and add the sea salt (use the best: *fleur de sel* or Maldon). Mix briefly and leave to draw out the moisture from the onions for 1 hour at room temperature, then blot the onions dry with a clean cloth or paper towels and set aside.

Horseradish vinaigrette

Mix the vinegar, salt, pepper, horseradish, and olive oil.

Baby fennel and radish salad

Pinch off the flowers from the bunch of fresh thyme.
Peel off the outermost layer from the baby fennel bulbs with a potato peeler and peel or scrub the radishes if wished. Slice very thinly, using a mandoline cutter, very sharp knife, or slicer attachment on a food processor. Add the prepared red onions and dress with horseradish vinaigrette to taste; sprinkle with the thyme flowers.

Cooking the langoustines

Lightly oil a griddle or heavy, nonstick skillet with olive oil, and when very hot sear the langoustines, turning once; season with salt and pepper.

To serve

Arrange the fennel and radish salad in the center of each plate. Surround with a thin ribbon of horseradish vinaigrette and place three langoustines on top of each serving of salad.

To peel the langoustines (also known as Dublin Bay prawns and Norway lobsterettes) quickly and easily, first pull off their heads. Slide the lower blade of a pair of small, pointed scissors under the center of the ventral (underside) section of the langoustine and cut along the shell toward the tail, which should be left attached for this recipe. Snip along the "back" of the shell also, exposing the intestinal tract for removal. Use your thumbs to push the cut edges gently apart, releasing the flesh. Freshly grated horseradish can be found in large supermarkets and good delicatessens, usually displayed with chilled goods or with relishes such as gherkins...

For the langoustines
12 medium-sized langoustines (Dublin Bay prawns)
1 red onion
best quality sea salt (*fleur de sel*, Maldon)
olive oil
salt, freshly ground white pepper

For the horseradish vinaigrette
1 tbsp sherry vinegar
scant 1 tsp freshly grated horseradish (see note at end of method)
4 tbsp olive oil
salt, freshly ground white pepper

For the baby fennel and radish salad
8 baby fennel bulbs
12 small pink and white, or red, radishes (preferably oblong variety)
2 small, mild red onions
small bunch of fresh flowering thyme

fish and seafood

Grilled bream fillets with sesame seed coating, slow-baked tomatoes with olives

2 very fresh, large bream (see
note at end of method),
filleted and skinned
1¾ cups balsamic vinegar
4 tbsp best quality, unrefined
sesame seed oil
½ cup slow-baked tomatoes
(recipe on p. 60)
¾ cup best quality, small
French olives, pitted
4 tbsp olive oil
½ cup toasted sesame seeds
salt, freshly ground pepper

To garnish
4 fresh mint leaves
12 fresh cilantro leaves

Reduce the vinegar over a gentle heat until it becomes syrupy (see page 60 for method). Mix the reduced vinegar with the sesame seed oil; chill this dressing in the refrigerator. Preheat the oven to 275 °F.

Chop the slow-baked tomatoes and the olives coarsely; mix them together in a heatproof bowl. Add 3 tablespoons of olive oil and warm gently over simmering water. Add a little salt and pepper if wished.

Do not allow the surface of the fish to become too dry; season both sides of each bream fillet with salt and pepper. Turn the fillets so that the side exposed by removing the skin is uppermost and sprinkle liberally with sesame seeds, pressing these down firmly so that they adhere. Heat a very little olive oil in a nonstick skillet and place the fillets in it, coated side down. Lightly brown on this one side only. Transfer to a lightly oiled, shallow baking sheet, coated side uppermost, and cook for 6 minutes (if the fillets are very thick, cook for 2–3 minutes longer).

To serve
Put 2 tablespoonfuls of the tomato and olive mixture in the center of each plate; place the bream fillets on top of this.

Use scissors to cut the mint and cilantro leaves into thin strips. Stir them into the vinaigrette and spoon this dressing all over the fillets.

In China and Japan, food grilled with sesame seeds is very popular: the nutty taste of the sesame seeds and oil is delicious. Mediterranean species of bream, each fish weighing 1¾ lb before filleting, such as royal, gilthead, dentex) would normally be used for this recipe; very fresh sea bream or porgy is a more readily available alternative. Make sure no stray scales are left behind on the fillets after skinning.

Broiled lobster in the shell, licorice flavored carrots, sea urchin coral, spice bread dressing

To serve 4

4 frozen Canadian lobsters, each weighing 1–1¼ lb thawed weight
olive oil

For the sea urchin cream
½ cup stiffly beaten cream
2 oz sea urchin coral
pinch of salt, ground pepper

For the court-bouillon
1 finely sliced carrot
1 medium onion, finely sliced
1 leek (green section only), finely sliced
1 celery stalk
1 bay leaf
1 sprig of fresh thyme
coarse sea salt

For the licorice carrots
20 baby carrots
½ stick/2 oz unsalted butter
2 tbsp superfine sugar
1 small, thin stick of unsweetened "hard" licorice
2 tbsp juices from roast meat
1 slice of pain d'épices (spiced honey bread), very finely crumbled
fresh lemon juice
sea salt, table salt, freshly ground pepper

To serve
2 short sections cut from a thin "hard" licorice stick

Sea urchin cream
If you are able to buy sea urchins, you will need several to yield enough "coral." Break up the coral with a fork; mix with the cream, adding a very small pinch of salt and a little pepper, and chill in the refrigerator.

Making the court-bouillon and poaching the lobsters
Bring plenty of water to a boil in a large, very deep stock pot or pan; add the vegetables and flavorings listed for the court-bouillon. Boil for approximately 20 minutes. Put the lobsters into the gently boiling court-bouillon and simmer for no longer than 3–4 minutes after the liquid returns to a gentle boil. Take them out of the court-bouillon and plunge them immediately into a large bowl of iced water (use ice cubes). Detach the heads from the rest of the lobsters; cut the tails lengthwise in half, along the center of their backs, slicing right through them using a heavy, sharp knife; loosen the flesh from the shell but do not detach it completely; set aside.

Licorice flavored carrots
Peel the carrots, leaving a very short length of their stalks attached; boil them in a large pan of salted water (allow a scant ½ oz of salt for each 1¾ pints of water) until tender but still with a little "bite" left in them; drain and refresh in iced water. Drain again and glaze them by frying them gently in a pan or deep skillet with half the butter, the sugar and the licorice stick. When they are lightly browned, transfer them to a heated dish; add the meat

juices (or diluted very good quality meat extract) to the pan and scrape with a wooden spoon over the heat to loosen the cooking deposits. Stir in the pain d'épices crumbs. Add the remaining butter (as a solid piece) and beat with a balloon whisk as it melts; season with salt and pepper and add a few drops of lemon juice. Set aside.

Grilled lobsters
Drizzle a little olive oil over the surfaces of the lobster flesh in the half shells; place them under a hot broiler until the flesh has firmed up and stiffened; do not cook for more than a few minutes or they will be dry and tough.

To serve
Arrange 5 carrots on each plate, coat with the reserved cooking juices; place a half lobster on their tapering ends, tip the flesh to one side in the shell, toward the thicker end of the carrots, allowing room to place a rounded spoonful of the sea urchin cream in the shell (see facing page); place a small piece of licorice on top of this scoop of cream and surround the lobster and carrots with a thin trickle of olive oil.

> This dish is a pleasure to look at, with the white, red-mottled lobster flesh resting on its scarlet shell. Serve these lightly cooked lobsters immediately they are ready.

Scallop brochettes with Serrano raw cured ham, grilled lettuce hearts, roasted tomatoes and balsamic dressing

To serve 4

For the scallop brochettes
24 very fresh scallops (white part only)
4 thin slices Spanish Serrano cured, raw ham
2 tbsp olive oil
8 wooden skewers or bamboo satay sticks

For the pan-roasted lettuce hearts
2 hearts of romaine
2 tbsp olive oil
salt, freshly ground pepper

For the vinaigrette
¾ cup reduced roasting juices from veal, beef or chicken
scant ½ cup balsamic vinegar (see p. 54 for reduction method)
scant ½ cup hazelnut oil
salt, freshly ground pepper

To serve
4 ripe, medium-sized tomatoes
olive oil
salt, freshly ground pepper
8 Parmesan cheese shavings (optional)

Cut each Serrano ham slice into 4 pieces. Assemble the brochettes, starting with a scallop and alternate with pieces of the ham: allow 3 scallops for each brochette and 2 pieces of ham. Rinse the lettuce hearts, drain well and blot dry with a clean cloth or paper towels; cut them into quarters.

Vinaigrette

Heat the roasting juices (very good quality meat or chicken essence, diluted, could be used if necessary); stir in the reduced balsamic vinegar and the hazelnut oil with a wooden spoon; season to taste.

Cooking the lettuces and brochettes

Heat a very little olive oil in the griddle pan or skillet and cook the lettuces over a fairly high heat, turning them several times; season them with salt and pepper and transfer to a heated dish. Heat a very little fresh olive oil in the griddle pan or skillet and when very hot cook the brochettes, allowing only a few seconds on each side to allow them to brown lightly and barely cook through.

To serve

Pan-roast the tomatoes for a few minutes in a little olive oil, in a covered pan.
Using oval plates if you have them, arrange 2 quarters of lettuce heart on each, with a tomato, sprinkle with the warm balsamic vinegar dressing. Place a brochette on top of the lettuce hearts and garnish, if wished, with a couple of Parmesan cheese shavings.

> If anything, these little romaine lettuce hearts taste better cooked than raw and they are widely available. Use the delicious bright orange coral from the scallops to add flavor and color to a seafood dish or a white fish recipe; it will keep for 24 hours if refrigerated.

Squid and Mediterranean vegetables seared à la plancha, lemon confit

For the seared squid
1¼ lb fresh, small squid
2 tbsp olive oil
salt, freshly ground pepper

For the lemon confit
2 untreated lemons
1 cup water
⅔ cup sugar

For the Mediterranean vegetables "à la plancha"
2 baby violet artichokes
juice of 1 lemon
1 red bell pepper
1 small zucchini
4 large, bulbous scallions
olive oil
salt, freshly ground pepper

For the lemon confit dressing
juice of 1 lemon
scant ½ cup olive oil
1 ripe, deep-red tomato
small bunch of chives
salt, freshly ground pepper

Clean and prepare the squid, rinsing them very thoroughly under cold running water; drain them on a clean cloth; chill them in the refrigerator until needed.

Lemon confit
Boil the water and sugar together to make a light sugar syrup. Rinse the lemons under the cold faucet and slice them very thinly without peeling them. Add these slices to the sugar syrup. Cook over a gentle heat until the lemon slices are translucent. Drain and set aside.

Mediterranean vegetables "à la plancha"
Clean, trim, and rinse all the vegetables. Prepare the artichokes using a very sharp, small knife to "turn" them (see method in recipe on page 38, first paragraph). As you prepare each artichoke, immediately rub it with lemon juice to prevent discoloration and then add to a bowl of cold water acidulated with lemon juice.
Peel the bell pepper with a potato peeler, removing only the thin outer skin; remove and discard the seeds, stalk, and pale parts inside before cutting the flesh into large, square pieces.
Cut the zucchini into rounds; trim the scallions (use small, imported fresh white onions still attached to their green stalks if available).

Lemon confit dressing
Chop the lemon slices with a heavy knife, place them in a salad bowl, add the lemon juice, the olive oil, and a little of the sugar syrup in which the lemons were cooked, and season with salt and pepper.

Blanch the tomato for a few seconds in boiling water, then drain and peel it; remove the seeds and cut the flesh into small dice. Chop or snip the chives finely. Add the chives and tomato to the lemon confit dressing.

Cooking vegetables and squid Spanish style "à la plancha" (searing)
Heat a griddle or a heavy skillet over a high heat, pour in a little olive oil, and brown the vegetables, cooking each type separately. Sprinkle them with salt and pepper and keep them hot.
Dry the surface of the griddle or skillet with paper towels; pour in a very little fresh olive oil and return to a high heat. Sear the squid so that they brown lightly but are only just cooked. You can use the tentacles as well as the bodies if you buy baby squid. Season with salt and pepper.

To assemble the dish
Arrange the vegetables on each plate, alternating the colors; place the squid on top and surround with lemon confit dressing.

> If overcooked, grilled squid will become very tough and chewy. Searing them for a very short time over a high heat until they are only just cooked through leaves them tender and brings out their flavor.

Fried white fish fillets, leeks and almonds vinaigrette, fresh white cheese shake

For the fried fish fillets

4 very fresh hake or
whiting fillets, each
weighing about 5 oz
3 tbsp all-purpose flour
2 tbsp olive oil
juice of ½ lemon
salt, freshly ground pepper

**For the fresh cream
cheese shake**

8 oz very soft, moist fromage
blanc or fromage frais
scant ½ cup milk
juice of ½ lemon
1 tbsp olive oil
salt, freshly ground white
pepper

For the leeks vinaigrette

24 thin, baby leeks
small bunch fresh mint
4 "petals" of slow-baked
tomato (see recipe on
p. 54)
3 tbsp olive oil
juice of 1 lemon
1 tbsp blanched almonds,
coarsely chopped
sea salt, table salt
freshly ground pepper

Fresh cheese shake

Process all the ingredients in a blender and chill in the refrigerator. Fromage frais or other very soft white, fresh cheeses such as demi-sel or Petit Suisse are all suitable.

Leeks vinaigrette

Trim the leeks, removing the outermost layer; wash thoroughly; tie them together in a bundle with two well-spaced pieces of string and boil for 2 minutes in a large pan of boiling water; allow 2 tbsp salt for each 1¾ pints water. Remove from the pan and lower into a large bowl of iced water (use ice cubes).
Blanch the mint leaves for a few seconds only in the salted boiling water; rinse under the cold faucet and blot dry with paper towels. Cut them into fairly broad strips. Dice the slow-baked tomatoes finely.
Mix the olive oil and the lemon juice.

Fish fillets

Pick out any remaining bones from the fish with tweezers. Coat the fillets lightly with flour, shaking off excess. Fry briefly in hot olive oil in a skillet, turning once; when they are cooked, sprinkle with the lemon juice and a little salt. Keep hot.

To serve

Drain the leeks and remove the string; reheat them gently over a low heat in a nonstick pan. Sprinkle with the vinaigrette, the mint leaves, diced tomato, and the almonds. Transfer 6 leeks to each plate, spoon the remaining vinaigrette and other ingredients from the pan over them. Place the fillet of fish to one side of the leeks and serve with a glass of the fresh cheese shake.

Careful timing is the essence of success for this simple recipe: the leeks should be tender but still crisp and the fish fillets should be just cooked through, still moist and firm. Use fromage blanc (very fresh white cheese) that is "sloppy," almost the consistency of yogurt, for this recipe.

Crunchy pineapple and shrimp fried sandwich with herb stuffing

For the crunchy pineapple and shrimp fried sandwich
12 large, pink shrimp
1 large pineapple
olive oil
salt, freshly ground pepper

For the herb stuffing
1 oven-baked white loaf
(i.e. not steam-baked)
approximately 1¼ cups milk
bunch of fresh cilantro
¾ cup olive oil
pinch of chili powder,
Espelette if possible
juice of ½ lemon
salt, freshly ground pepper

For the caramelized balsamic vinegar
3 cups balsamic vinegar

For the egg and breadcrumb coating
2 tbsp all-purpose flour
2 eggs
2–3 heaped tbsp freshly made breadcrumbs (see method)
salt, freshly ground pepper

Cut all the crust away from a slightly stale white loaf; spread the crusts out on a baking sheet and dry in the oven (at 210 °F) until dry and crunchy. Reduce to fine breadcrumbs in a food processor. Meanwhile break up the soft inside of the loaf into fairly small pieces and place in a bowl. Add sufficient milk to cover and leave to soak.

Peel the pineapple and cut 8 thin, rectangular slices measuring 3 x 1½ inches. Place these on paper towels on a large plate and sprinkle lightly with salt to draw out their excess moisture. Set aside.

Caramelized balsamic vinegar
Reduce the balsamic vinegar in a heavy-bottomed pan over a gentle heat until it becomes syrupy and coats the bottom of the pan lightly when tipped to one side.

Herb bread stuffing
Place the cilantro leaves, the olive oil, and a pinch of salt in the food processor and blend. Squeeze out excess moisture from the milk-soaked bread and add to the mixture, with the chili pepper powder; process until very well blended and uniformly pale green. Add a little lemon juice, and more seasoning if needed. If the mixture is very stodgy, add a very little milk and process briefly.

Crunchy pineapple, shrimp sandwich
Blot dry the rectangles of pineapple with fresh paper towels; use a knife to spread a thin layer of the herb stuffing over the pineapple slices. Cook the shrimp briefly in a little hot olive oil over a high heat, season with a little salt and pepper, and blot dry on paper towels. Cut the shrimp lengthwise in two, or three, depending on their size. Spread them out evenly on half the pineapple slices. Cover with remaining slices and press lightly so the shrimp are securely sandwiched between two layers of herb stuffing.

Coating and frying the sandwiches
Spread the flour out on a large plate; beat the eggs lightly and pour into another, deeper, plate; spread the home-made breadcrumbs out on a third plate. Carefully coat each sandwich all over with flour, then dip in the beaten egg; finally coat with breadcrumbs. Have 2 tablespoons of very hot olive oil ready in a large, nonstick skillet; fry the sandwiches on both sides until they are well browned.

To serve
Surround each sandwich with a trickle of the caramelized balsamic vinegar.

Make sure the crusts are totally dried out before you make the breadcrumbs in the food processor; if you have made more than you need for the "sandwiches," store in an airtight jar: home-made breadcrumbs are much better than store-bought ones.
If you use North Sea shrimp which are smaller, double the quantity. Buy unpeeled shrimp and peel them yourself: they have more flavor.

Southern Mediterranean

Lapping the shores of the Maghreb, the Mediterranean makes its geographical landfall in North Africa while coming into contact with the East by an accident of history. The western part of North Africa has frequently been invaded and here disparate peoples, languages, ways of life, and religions have lived side by side—and sometimes clashed: Berbers, Kabyles, Phoenicians, Greeks, Romans, Arabs, Turks, Jews, Christians, Muslims, and later the French colonists. This cultural brew has rendered the Maghreb one of the most complex regions in the world. It is only natural that its gastronomy should reflect this complexity, mirroring the cultural layers piled on top of one another, like the many layers of pastry in a *pastilla*. It also reflects the country's varying climate: hot near the coast, more bracing in the foothills of the Atlas mountains and on the plateaux, harsh in the heart of the high mountains. Then there is the desert, covering a vast area of Morocco, Algeria, and

Above: *the souk or great central market in Marrakech.*
Facing page, left:
these Far-Eastern paper lanterns add to the oriental ambiance at the Compagnie des Comptoirs.

Above: *sweetened tea with fresh mint is much more than a culinary tradition in Morocco. It is part of the ritual of social intercourse, a courtesy always extended to guest and friend alike, and to accept and appreciate its taste and scent is an indispensable part of any relationship.*

southern Tunisia. This region's culinary traditions also reflect the richness and diversity of its flora and fauna: the coastal seas are full of fish—Agadir is the world's most important sardine-fishing port—while goats and sheep graze the upland pastures, and down in the plains olive and orange groves, vineyards, and orchards stretch out over the landscape.

Liquid gold and aromatics

Of all Maghreb cuisines, we find Moroccan cooking the most fascinating. Morocco is a world apart, safeguarding the treasures of its ancient history through a culture that is highly evolved, secretive, and sometimes disconcerting: hidden among the high valleys of the Atlas or in the innermost palace courtyards, it demands perseverance to discover. Once the threshold has been crossed, however, what cultural riches are revealed! Moroccan hospitality is informed by age-old custom, starting with a welcome of bread and *amlou* (almond paste sweetened with honey and flavored with argan oil). Argan oil is a product unique to Morocco, typical of the Sous plain, Agadir, Essaouira, and Taroudannt, extracted from the nuts of the wild argan tree that grows only in the south of Morocco. Rare and much sought after, it has an enchanting, musky aroma. Production of the oil is still a cottage industry, in which only women are involved. The other liquid gold treasure of Morocco is olive oil; Moroccan cooking does indeed seem to be typified by various shades of gold. Those precious golden oils, oranges and lemons, spices such as turmeric that imparts its color to the aromatic spice mixture *ras-el-hanout*, and, above all, saffron—all find their place in the royal tradition of cooking. These glimmers of gold give Moroccan cuisine its vivid, colorful appearance, enhancing the freshness of the vegetables which are the particular pride of Fez, offsetting the purity and blandness of couscous and highlighting the delicious aromas of meats that have been slow-cooked in tajines with honey, spices, preserved lemons, dates, and dried fruits. The *pastilla*, a pie made with flaky pastry, filled with a sweet-savory mixture of onions, pigeon, hard-boiled eggs, and almonds, symbolizes all the splendor of this palace gastronomy, prepared by highly skilled cooks.

The delights of paradise lost

Such a rich culinary tradition, so full of scents and aromas, which delicately combines the savory and the sweet, has been nourished, in common with other great cuisines, by foreign influences and by the contributions of immigrants far back in time. Drawing on two thousand years of history, Morocco's gastronomy was born when the native Berber cuisine came into contact with the aristocratic tradition of medieval Andalusia, that Spanish paradise lost, mourned in the hearts of Muslims, a golden age that preceded the *Reconquista*, when the south of the Iberian peninsula was reconquered during the fifteenth century by the Catholic monarchs Ferdinand and Isabella. After the reconquest, many Muslims who were forced to leave Spain took refuge in Morocco while, at the same time, the Sephardic Jews who had also been expelled from Spain brought with them their knowledge of the art of eating well. This era, known as "Al Andalus," persists to this day in the folk memory of the Maghrebians as a golden age when tolerance and civilization were a way of life, when science—particularly the branch of medicine—flourished and the cuisine of the region was one of the most exquisite ever known. But of course this perfection was not a product of spontaneous generation. The Andalusians had themselves borrowed a great deal from the East, especially from Persia and from Byzantium—notably the essentials of their dietary and culinary principles: the sweet-savory mixtures; combining meat and poultry with fresh fruits and with dried fruits; simmering over very low heat; the use of honey, of cinnamon, saffron, and scented waters such as rose water and orange-flower water, all of which originated from Persia. This is yet another example of how such cuisines, apparently steeped in immutable tradition, have developed as a result of travel and cultural cross-fertilization.

Above: *a grocer and spice merchant's stall, around 1919, in a souk, or market in Fez. A traditional, unchanging choice of aromatic and appetizing foodstuffs: spices, dates, garlands of figs, and all sorts of flours and cereals.*

Roast lamb shanks and salsify purée with hazelnut milk, rich gravy, and crushed hazelnuts

For the lamb shanks
4 lamb shanks
2 tbsp grapeseed oil
2 carrots, finely sliced
1 medium onion, finely sliced
1 leek, white part only, finely sliced
thyme, bay leaf
4 cups chicken stock
1 tbsp sherry vinegar
1½ tbsp butter

For the salsify purée
12 oz salsify
juice of 1 lemon
1 white, floury potato
1½ tbsp butter
pinch of sugar
salt, freshly ground white pepper

To garnish
½ cup whole hazelnuts

For the hazelnut milk
scant ½ cup whole milk
1 tbsp light cream
1 tbsp hazelnut oil
salt, freshly ground pepper

For the salad
3½ oz baby spinach leaves
1 tbsp sherry vinegar
2 tbsp walnut oil
salt, freshly ground pepper

Braised lamb shanks

Preheat the oven to 195 °F.

Brown the lamb shanks all over in the olive oil in a large, fairly deep, fireproof casserole dish; add all the flavoring ingredients listed up to, and including, the thyme and bay leaf. Stir and turn and fry gently for 2 minutes before adding the chicken stock and bring to a boil. Transfer to the preheated oven and cook for 2½ hours. Drain all the liquid and juices from the cooked lamb into a bowl for later use. Place the lamb shanks under a hot grill to caramelize their surfaces.

Salsify purée

Prepare a large bowl of cold water acidulated with plenty of lemon juice, and as you peel each salsify root cut it into short lengths and place immediately in this bowl to prevent discoloration. Cook the salsify with the peeled and chopped potato in a little water with the butter and sugar in a heavy-bottomed pan. When the salsify and the potatoes are very tender (this will take about 30 minutes), drain and process to a very smooth purée in the food processor. Season to taste.

Garnish

Roast the hazelnuts for about 10 minutes on a baking sheet in the oven, preheated to 350 °F. Rub off their fine, papery skins in a clean cloth. Crush them coarsely.

Hazelnut milk

Mix the milk, cream, and hazelnut oil in a pan. Place over a low heat and season with salt and pepper. Before serving, blend the mixture with a hand-held electric beater.

Rich gravy

Transfer one-quarter of the cooking juices reserved from baking the lamb shanks to a pan and reduce over a moderate heat, uncovered, until thickened to a syrupy, glossy consistency. Add the sherry vinegar, followed by the extra piece of butter. Use a hand-held electric beater to blend the butter into the gravy as it melts. Add salt and pepper to taste.

The salad

Wash and dry the baby spinach leaves, discarding any wilted or damaged leaves; toss them in the vinaigrette of sherry vinegar, walnut oil, salt, and pepper.

To serve

Use 2 tablespoons to shape an oval "quenelle" or dumpling of the salsify puree and place on one side of each plate. Position the spinach salad on the other side and place the lamb shank between them. Add a little hazelnut milk and, near the shank, some of the gravy. Sprinkle with the crushed toasted hazelnuts.

> If you want to make the lamb shanks look particularly mouth watering, make a caramel with a scant ½ cup superfine sugar and when this has melted and started to color, add a little soy sauce. Brush the cooked, drained knuckle all over with this mixture and then place under a very hot broiler, turning regularly, to glaze.

Steak parillada "smashed" potatoes; red wine, shallot, and anchovy sauce

To serve 4

For the steak *parillada*
4 thick, well-hung, mature prime beef entrecôte steaks
large bunch of fresh white onions (see note)
2 limes
olive oil
salt, freshly ground black pepper
8 wooden skewers for brochettes

For the red wine, shallot, and anchovy sauce
4 shallots
¼ stick/1 oz butter + 1½ tbsp to finish sauce
1 cup good quality dry red wine
1 cup beef stock, preferably homemade, reduced
4 anchovy fillets (preserved in oil)
salt, freshly ground pepper

For the "smashed" potatoes
1¼–1½ lb yellow, waxy, or salad potatoes
3 tbsp olive oil
salt, freshly ground black pepper

To serve
2 tbsp olive oil
best quality sea salt (*fleur de sel*, Maldon)

Wash the potatoes and boil them, unpeeled, until tender in plenty of boiling salted water.

Red wine, shallot, and anchovy sauce
Peel and chop the shallots very finely. Cook them very gently in ¼ stick/1 oz) butter until soft but not at all browned. Add the red wine and simmer, uncovered, until all the moisture has evaporated. Add the beef stock and reduce to half its original volume over a low heat. Finish the sauce by adding the anchovies, crushed with a fork, and when they have dissolved add the remaining small piece of butter, beating with a balloon whisk as it melts into the sauce.

Grilled steak
Peel off the outer layer of the fresh white onions (see note at end of method), trim off the roots and about two-thirds of the stem but leave the onions whole. Reserve 4 of them to garnish the finished dish. Cut the limes lengthwise into quarters. Cut the entrecôte steaks into large pieces (slightly bigger than normal bite size) and thread them on to the skewers, starting with a lime quarter, followed by a piece of steak, then a whole white onion and so on. Prepare 2 brochettes per person.

"Smashed" potatoes
Peel and place potatoes in a large bowl; use a potato masher or large fork to break them up roughly but do not mash them. Season with salt and pepper; stir in the olive oil. Keep hot.

Grilling the steak
Cook the remaining onions in olive oil in a heavy-bottomed pan, until they are very tender and golden brown. Season with a little salt and pepper and set aside.

Heat a little olive oil in a very wide heavy, nonstick skillet or use a griddle; when hot add the brochettes and cook, turning once or twice; cooking time will depend on how rare or well-done you prefer your steak.

To serve
Spoon some of the potatoes onto each plate, garnish with the braised, whole onions. Add the steak brochettes. Pour a thin trickle of red wine, shallot, and anchovy sauce around the contents of the plate, add a trickle of olive oil and sprinkle a pinch of very good sea salt over each brochette.

This is a robust dish inspired by the *parilladas* so beloved by the Argentinos, for which full-flavored meat from young, entire bulls is used, and it is also a reminder of the bullring at Nîmes, and of the Camargue. This recipe is also delicious if the more tender, well-hung entrecôte beefsteak comes from a castrated animal. Use fresh white onions, with large bulbs and their stalks still attached. Large, bulbous scallions may be substituted, as may home-grown fresh shallots, to imitate the authentic young onions grown around Lézignan in France.

Chicken and chili pepper tortilla wrap
with plain yogurt and cilantro

To serve 4

For the sautéed chicken

4 chicken breasts, skinned
pinch of chili pepper
powder (Espelette)
olive oil
salt, freshly ground pepper

For the vegetables

4 large scallions or fresh
white onions
1 red bell pepper, skinned
4 oz button mushrooms
1 zucchini
1 fresh white onion,
with stalk, or large scallion,
or fresh shallot
small bunch of fresh cilantro
olive oil
salt, freshly ground pepper

To assemble the dish

4 plain corn tortillas (soft)
2 slices raw cured ham
(lean, coarser quality
prosciutto type)
4 tbsp plain yogurt
4 slow-cooked tomato 'petals'
(see recipe on p. 54)
1 lime, cut lengthwise into
quarters
best sea salt (*fleur
de sel*, Maldon),
freshly ground pepper
olive oil

Preheat the oven to 325 °F.

Cut each tortilla into 3 equal parts; shape each in turn by pressing it over a fairly large pastry cutter or similar utensil, molding the tortilla into a "cup" shape (see facing page). Place these in the oven to dry for approximately 10 minutes to "set" their shape, then keep ready for use in a warm, dry place.

Place the ham slices in a wide, nonstick skillet, place some nonstick paper on top of them and then weight down with another skillet or pan of the same or slightly smaller diameter. Dry very gently over a very low heat for about 15 minutes; the object is to make the ham very crisp and crunchy—you will need to check it from time to time. Place the crisp (but not at all burnt) ham in the food processor and reduce to a powdery consistency.

Slice the chicken breasts into thick strips. Place them in a bowl and sprinkle them all over with the chili powder; add seasoning and leave to flavor for 30 minutes.

The vegetables

Wash, trim, and peel all the vegetables. Cut the red bell pepper into fairly wide julienne strips (having discarded the seeds and inner pith etc.); cut the mushrooms into quarters and dice the zucchini. Slice or chop the onion very finely. Take the cilantro leaves off their stalks.

Cooking the chicken and vegetables

Heat 2 nonstick skillets. Pour a very little olive oil into each of them. Gently fry the chicken strips in 1 pan, allowing them to brown lightly; cook the vegetables, one type at a time, in the other pan, starting with the zucchini. Fry the mushrooms and allow them to brown lightly; do likewise with the fresh white onion or scallions (or your chosen substitute) and with the red bell pepper. Season to taste. Mix all these ingredients with the chicken and add the cilantro leaves.

To serve

Place 3 pieces of tortilla on each plate, concave side uppermost; spoon the chicken and vegetable mixture neatly into each tortilla section. Add 1 tablespoon of plain yogurt to each serving, sprinkle with some of the powdered raw, cured ham, and decorate with a tomato petal and a lime quarter. Sprinkle with some best quality sea salt, some freshly ground pepper, and surround with a trickle of olive oil.

> The technique of drying out the ham slices is almost the same as for the bream skin (see method on page 70): the slices have to be laid out absolutely flat against the bottom of the nonstick skillet; cover if wished with greaseproof paper and place another pan on top to keep the slice flat against the surface of the hot pan. When ready, the ham should be dry and crunchy, rather like a crisp, but not discoloured. The tortillas are dried to shape to serve the same purpose as tacos and have an agreeably crisp texture.

Eastern Mediterranean

When a native of southern Europe speaks of the eastern Mediterranean, the reference is not simply

to a distant region but also to a mother country. Down the centuries, the Levant and the Occident

have reached out toward each other. During the sixth century BC many trading posts were founded

by Greek settlers along the coastline of what was to become southern Gaul, at Agde, Marseilles,

Hyères, Antibes, Nice; and inland, at Arles and Glanum, and, later, at Aleria in Corsica. Greeks and

Phoenicians were for centuries engaged in maritime commerce. The Greek presence in the eastern

Mediterranean was relatively short lived, but left traces that are still discernible today, especially in

the cooking of the area. Saffron, transported throughout the ancient world by the Phoenicians and

highly prized by the Greeks, had already become the world's rarest and most costly spice. It is still

an essential ingredient in traditional recipes such as *tielle*, a specialty of Sète (a pie made with

Above: *Istanbul is usually thought of as the gateway between East and West: an orange sun glows above a boat cruising along the Bosphorus, silhouetted against the coastline of the Turkish capital.*
Facing page: *dried small chiles, ready to add fierce, peppery heat to eastern Mediterranean dishes.*

Left: *succulent fresh vegetables, bursting with sunshine, displayed in an eastern Mediterranean market.* Right: *in a pool at the Compagnie des Comptoirs' premises, a water lily conjures up thoughts of secret gardens in harems, the fountains of Ottoman palaces, and the graceful Egyptian lotus.*

saffron-flavored and colored cuttlefish), bouillabaisse, and rouille. Aioli, which has long been part of the Italian, Spanish, and Provençal repertoires, originated in Greece, where it is called *skordhalia* and is served with poached fish and vegetables. Other versions of this cold, garlic-flavored sauce are found in Turkish, Syrian, and Egyptian cooking, one example being *tarator*, which may also contain sesame paste, pounded almonds or walnuts, breadcrumbs, and yogurt, or can simply be made with crushed garlic blended with a little oil, as in the Syrian version.

Origins of bouillabaisse and the Levantine sweet tooth

The bouillabaisse of Marseilles has a Greek ancestor that survives to this day in the form of *kakavia*, a more primitive recipe than its descendant: a selection of fish, including bream, John Dory, moray eel, conger eel, and grouper, is simply boiled gently over a low heat with vegetables and potatoes. The soup and the fish are served together as one dish.

For many years the flavors of the eastern Mediterranean have tended to travel westward. The sophisticated cuisine of Muslim Andalusia was widely renowned in the Middle Ages, being a synthesis of Persian, Arabic, and Byzantine influences. Through its recipes the methods and dietary customs of earliest antiquity were passed on to later generations. Subsequently it was the turn of the Ottoman Empire, as the Turks' conquests multiplied and their trading ports proliferated in the Balkans and North Africa, to spread the culinary expertise of the sultans' cooks, as well as the customs and practices contributed by Byzantine cooking, which had in turn benefited from the legacy of ancient Greece. Those soft and yielding pieces of Turkish delight (*loukoum*) with their aroma of rose petals, pistachio, or mastic; the wafer-thin sheets of phyllo wheat pastry used to make crisp, crunchy sweetmeats; and *kadaif* (very fine vermicelli-like strands of pastry) are found in Turkey, Greece, Syria and the Lebanon, in Egypt, and throughout the Maghreb. The confection of Middle-Eastern pastries involves alternating sheets of phyllo pastry or layers of *kadaif* (that have been liberally coated with melted butter) with layers of crushed almonds, pistachios, hazelnuts, or other ingredients. Once these pastries have been baked in the oven, they are sprinkled all over with sugar syrup scented with rose petals or orange blossom. They are the inspiration for our own oriental pastries made with pears and almonds. The pleasure of tasty morsels or nibbles is a quintessentially Mediterranean experience. In Spain and Italy, wines and aperitifs are accompanied by *tapas* or *antipasti*, while in the eastern Mediterranean region great importance is attached to similar traditional delicacies. In Turkey these "little dishes" are known as *meze*, in Syria and Lebanon as *mezze*, in Greece *mezedhes,* and in North Africa *kemia*. As with *tapas*, there are countless *meze* recipes, ranging from the simple and unadorned olive or slice of turnip pickled in brine to complex and highly spiced preparations using vegetables, meat, and seafood.

Olive oil: from amphorae to earthenware jars and bottles

The eastern Mediterranean is where Orient and Occident meet. No one seems to know exactly where the boundary lies. Perhaps in Greece, whose culture has a great many oriental characteristics, discernible in its music, poetry, and food. Or maybe in Turkey, resolutely Asian but preoccupied by Europe after centuries of intertwined history. One certainty, however, remains: olive oil is the golden thread that runs through all Mediterranean civilizations, with the olive branch being synonymous with peace. Archeological digs in the area are still unearthing the two-handled, large earthenware jars used for centuries to store olive oil. These lands are home to almond, fig, orange, and lemon trees (providing the raw materials for preserved or candied fruits); grape vines, wild herbs, aromatic resins, incense, honey, and beeswax. It is customary for the inhabitants to sit in the shade outside their local café and put the world to rights over an aniseed-flavored drink. This is a world where time moves slowly, like a lazy trickle of olive oil down the side of an earthenware jar.

A spice merchant carefully weighs out some of his precious stock in the Khan and Khaliby souk in Cairo.

Broiled fillet steaks, Montpellier butter, onion compote, beet chips

4 tournedos (filet mignon
beef fillet steaks) about
5–6 oz each
4 strips of dry-cured
smoked bacon
best quality sea salt

For the onion compote
6 mild white onions
1½ tbsp butter
½ cup superfine sugar
3½ tbsp balsamic vinegar
table salt, best quality sea
salt, freshly ground pepper

For the Montpellier sauce
bunch of watercress
bunch flat-leaf parsley
small bunch chervil
small bunch chives
2 oz baby spinach leaves,
blanched and drained
4 shallots, peeled and minced
4 small gherkins
2 anchovy fillets
2 tbsp capers
3 small garlic cloves
1 egg yolk
pinch of Cayenne pepper
(optional)
1¾ sticks/7 oz butter, softened
salt, ground white pepper

For the beet chips
1 raw beet, peeled
2¾ cups superfine sugar
4 cups water

Onion compote

Slice the onions very finely and cook gently in the butter over a low heat. When they become translucent (do not allow to brown), add the sugar and the balsamic vinegar. Continue cooking slowly until the vinegar has evaporated. Continue cooking over the lowest possible heat, stirring now and then, for about 1 hour. The onions should have reduced to a very soft, mushy consistency; remove from the heat, season to taste.

Montpellier butter

Take all the fresh herb leaves off their stems; place all the ingredients except for the butter in a food processor and process to a paste. Add the butter and process until the mixture is light and "fluffy." Set aside in a cool place.

Beet chips

Preheat the oven to 250 °F. Cut the beet into very thin slices. Heat the water and sugar and boil briefly to make a light syrup. Add the wafer-thin beet slices to the syrup, allow them to soak in it for a few minutes, then remove them and spread out in a single layer on nonstick wax or silicone paper on a baking sheet. Put them in the oven to dry out and crisp for approximately 1 hour.

Cooking and serving

Dry-fry the bacon strips in a nonstick skillet until it is very crisp. Keep hot.

Broil the steaks, or fry them in a very little oil: the cooking time will depend on how rare you like your steak. Sprinkle with a little sea salt when cooked. Heat the Montpellier butter with a very little water in a small pan and then blend with a hand-held electric mixer. Spoon some of the onion compote onto each plate, place a steak on top and pour some of the Montpellier butter sauce around and on top of each steak. Garnish with beet chips and with the crisp bacon.

> Montpellier butter is a very old sauce recipe that is usually served with broiled fish and various types of cold meat. Some recipes include the anchovies, some not, but plenty of fresh herbs are always essential. In our part of France, we always make the onion compote with local onions, from Lézignan: large, fresh, white onions that have a particularly sweet taste when cooked slowly for a long time. Use the mildest onions you can buy and, if necessary, cheat by adding a pinch of superfine sugar.

La Compagnie's warm, cool, and Arctic cappuccino; brownies

To serve 4

For the thick hot chocolate
6½ oz best quality unsweetened plain or bitter chocolate
3½ oz milk chocolate
1¼ cups milk
⅔ cup light cream

For the vanilla-flavored Chantilly cream
2 cups whipping cream
¾ cup confectioners' sugar
½ vanilla bean

For the coffee granita
2 cups hot espresso coffee
⅓ cup hot, diluted chicory essence
4 tbsp superfine sugar

For the brownies
¾ stick/3 oz unsalted butter + 2 tsp extra for the baking pan
1 scant cup all-purpose flour + 1 tsp extra for the baking pan
1½ cups superfine sugar
4 eggs
6 tbsp pure, unsweetened cocoa powder
1 cup pecan nuts, coarsely chopped
½ cup good quality chocolate drops or chips

Decorate with
4 fresh mint leaves
1 tbsp coarsely crushed cocoa beans

Thick chocolate (warm ganache)

Chop the two types of chocolate and mix them together in a heatproof bowl. Bring the milk and cream to a boil, pour this onto the chopped chocolate. Stir carefully with a wooden spoon until completely smooth and glossy. Keep warm over hot (not boiling) water.

Vanilla-flavored Chantilly cream

Mix the cream and the confectioners' sugar, stir in the seeds from the half vanilla bean (slit the bean and scrape out the seeds with the tip of a knife). Pour through a very fine mesh strainer. Chill in a bowl. When very cold, beat until stiff with a hand-held electric beater; return to the refrigerator.

Coffee granita

Mix all the ingredients while the coffee is still hot. Leave to cool completely; place in the freezer. Just before serving the "cappuccino," break up the frozen mixture by running the prongs of a fork along the surface, resulting in coffee ice crystals.

Making and baking the brownies

Preheat the oven to 350 °F. Use the extra butter to grease a fairly deep rectangular cake pan; dust the greased pan with the extra flour, tipping out excess. Beat the butter vigorously with the superfine sugar until very pale and light, beat in the eggs one by one and then stir in the sifted flour and cocoa. Fold in the pecan nuts and the chocolate drops. Turn this cake mixture into the prepared cake pan and bake for 30–35 minutes or until a skewer inserted into it comes out clean. The brownie cake should be fairly firm when done but still moist and almost "fluffy"; remove from the oven and cut into squares in the pan while hot. Leave to cool a little and take them out of the pan while they are still slightly warm. They will turn "fudgy" as they cool.

Assembling the warm, cool, and Arctic cappuccino

Fill each of 4 glasses one-third full with the thick, warm chocolate; fill the next third with a layer of Chantilly cream; spoon the coffee granita on top of this. Decorate with a mint leaf and crushed cocoa beans. Serve on a plate, placing 2 brownie squares beside each cappuccino.

> This dessert will delight chocaholics. You can substitute walnuts for pecans. Crushed cocoa beans can be bought in stores specializing in confectioners' ingredients and high quality chocolate products.

Grand Marnier and marron glacé frozen soufflé with hot hazelnut frothy topping; chocolate-coated coffee ice-cream popsicles

For the frozen soufflé
2 cups whipping cream
4 tbsp superfine sugar + 1
cup sugar for the sugar syrup
¾ cup raw egg whites
(approximately 7 egg whites)
9 oz unsweetened chestnut
marron glacé purée
3½ tbsp Grand Marnier

**For the hot hazelnut
frothy topping**
4 tbsp superfine sugar
½ cup hazelnuts
3½ tbsp light pouring cream
or whipping cream

**For the chocolate-coated
coffee ice-cream
popsicles**
2½ leaves gelatin
3 tbsp best quality
unsweetened cocoa powder
2 tbsp superfine sugar
1 cup espresso coffee
(or strong instant coffee)
14 oz Menier or other best
quality European dark
chocolate to coat the
popsicles
small popsicle moulds

Decorate with
pure cocoa powder or best
drinking chocolate powder

Grand Marnier and marron glacé frozen soufflé

Beat the cream until it is very firm and stands up in peaks. Chill in the refrigerator.

Heat the cup of superfine sugar with 4½ tbsp water in a small, lipped pan with a thick base over a moderate heat until it boils; cook until it reaches a temperature of 250 °F (large ball stage). Beat the egg whites stiffly in a very large bowl preferably with a fixed rotary beater. Beat in 4 tbsp superfine sugar to make the egg whites even firmer. Add the hot syrup, pouring it in a very thin stream while beating the egg whites continuously. The resulting meringue mixture should be smooth and glossy; it is called Italian meringue. Leave to become completely cold.

Mix the marron purée with the Grand Marnier and then fold carefully into the cold Italian meringue. Fold in the stiffly beaten cream. Spoon an equal amount of this mixture into tall, freezer-proof glass tumblers and freeze.

Hazelnut froth

Heat the sugar in a small, heavy-bottomed pan until it melts and caramelizes to a light brown color. Add the hazelnuts and stir well. Add the cream and bring to a boil. Leave for 30 minutes, to cool to lukewarm; pour into the blender, process at high speed and strain through a fine strainer. Keep hot in the top section of a double boiler or in a bowl, over gently simmering water.

Chocolate-coated coffee ice-cream popsicles

Soften the gelatin leaves by soaking them in a bowl of cold water for 5 minutes.

Mix the cocoa powder and the sugar in a heatproof bowl and add the coffee. Add the gelatin and stir. When it has completely dissolved, pour the mixture into small popsicle molds with the sticks already in place; freeze until solid. Melt the chocolate in a heatproof bowl over hot water, unmold the deep-frozen popsicles and dip them in it, one by one, returning them to the freezer once coated.

To serve

Take the tumblers out of the freezer. Beat the hazelnut mixture until it is very frothy indeed with a hand-held electric beater. Spoon the froth into the tumblers, sprinkle a little cocoa or drinking chocolate powder on top and serve accompanied by the chocolate-coated ice-cream popsicles.

> This dessert makes the most of the chestnut's natural affinity with chocolate and hazelnuts.
> The hazelnut froth adds a wonderfully light topping that begins to melt the feather-light frozen meringue mixture beneath it. This is a dramatic dessert to serve at the end of a meal.

Crunchy chocolate and raspberry nems, vanilla-flavored mascarpone

For the crunchy fried *nems*
6 spring roll wrappers (see note on p. 162)
2 cups raspberries
1 egg yolk, lightly beaten
4 cups light olive oil or sunflower-seed oil for frying
confectioners' sugar

For the chocolate cream (ganache)
⅔ cup whole milk
⅔ cup light, pouring cream
2 egg yolks
2 tbsp superfine sugar
4 oz *couverture* (see note at end of method), coarsely chopped

For the mascarpone cream
1 cup whipping cream
1 cup Italian mascarpone
scant ½ cup confectioners' sugar
1 vanilla bean, slit open

For the chocolate cream (ganache) decoration
¾ cup heavy cream
7 oz dark, sweetened cooking chocolate (e.g. Menier), coarsely chopped

To assemble the dessert
¾–1 cup purée of mixed red berry fruit

The chocolate cream (ganache)
Bring the milk and cream slowly to a boil. Remove from the heat. Beat the egg yolks with the sugar until very pale and light; keep beating continuously as you add the hot milk and cream a little at a time. Return to a very low heat and cook while stirring with a wooden spatula until the custard thickens somewhat; do not allow to boil or it will curdle. Use a double boiler if preferred. Remove from the heat, add the chopped chocolate, and stir gently as the chocolate melts, making sure that it blends evenly into the custard. Pour the custard into small tumblers, until they are half full.

The mascarpone cream
Beat the whipping cream stiffly. Mix the mascarpone with the sugar in a fairly large bowl. Use a pointed knife to scrape the sticky seeds from inside the vanilla bean into the sweetened mascarpone. Fold in the beaten cream.

Chocolate cream (ganache)
Bring the cream to a boil, remove it from the heat, add the chocolate, stir gently but thoroughly, and leave to cool. Use 2 teaspoons or coffee spoons to shape little "eggs" or a melon-scoop to shape balls of chocolate cream, to be used as part of the filling for the *nems*. Chill these in the refrigerator.

Crunchy nems
Heat the oil (light olive oil or sunflower-seed oil) to 350 °F.
Cut each spring roll wrapper (5 x 5 inches) in half and wrap each strip (5 x 2½ inches)

securely around a few raspberries and one of the little chocolate dumplings, enveloping them completely, rather like little Vietnamese spring rolls or *nems*; seal the edges of the nem securely together by brushing with beaten egg yolk. Use a frying basket and lower the *nems* into the very hot oil to fry briefly until they are pale golden brown; drain and dust with sifted confectioners' sugar.

Assembling the dessert
Working quickly, distribute the *nems* evenly between the tumblers containing the chocolate custard, top with some of the vanilla-flavored mascarpone cream and drizzle a little red berry purée on top. Serve at once.

> Timing is very important when frying these sweet *nems*: they should be a pale golden color and crisp but the contents inside should not be subjected to much heat. *Couverture* chocolate, sold to confectioners and to restaurants and so on, usually has to be bought in large quantities. Good quality unsweetened dark cooking chocolate can be substituted.

Honeyed eggplant crisp with frothy lemon sorbet

Crisp topping

Mix together the flour, confectioners' sugar, and ground almonds. Melt the butter and pour it over this mixture. Use the tips of your fingers to carry out a version of "rubbing in" until the mixture looks like fine breadcrumbs. Chill in the refrigerator.

Honeyed eggplant

Cut the eggplant flesh into dice approximately ⅜ inch square. Bring the Muscat wine to a boil with the honey. Add the seeds from the split vanilla bean (scraped out with the sharp point of a knife) and the diced eggplant. Cook over a low heat. When the diced eggplant is very tender, add the lemon juice. Set aside.

Frothy lemon sorbet

Make a sugar syrup by heating the sugar and water; when it has boiled, leave it to cool. Add the freshly-opened, effervescent Perrier water to the cold syrup. Add the egg whites and mix them gently with the lemon-flavored syrup. Freeze in a sorbetière or ice-cream maker.

Caramelized Banyuls wine

Reduce the wine slowly until it reaches a syrupy consistency.

Cooking and serving

Preheat the oven to 350 °F. You will need 6 flan or tart rings, nonstick if possible, approximately 5 inches in diameter; place these on a nonstick baking sheet and pack them three-quarters full with the eggplant mixture. Add an even layer of crisp topping and bake in the oven until lightly browned (approximately 20 minutes). To serve, put a large spatula under each ring and its contents and carefully transfer to a plate; remove the ring. Garnish with an oval or round scoop of sorbet and surround with some of the caramelized Banyuls wine.

> A pudding made with aubergines? Try it! You will discover something novel and delicious. Sweet dishes and confectionary made with eggplant are very popular in the eastern Mediterranean; in Greece tiny whole eggplant cooked in syrup are sometimes served to welcome a visitor, accompanying a drink or coffee.

To serve 6

6 flan or tart rings 5 inches in diameter

For the crisp
⅛ cup all-purpose flour
scant ½ cup confectioners' sugar
⅔ cup ground almonds
½ stick/2 oz butter

For the honeyed eggplant
1¾ lb eggplant flesh
5 tbsp lavender honey
1½ cups Muscat de Frontignan (good quality French Muscat grape dessert wine)
1 vanilla bean
juice of 1 lemon

For the frothy sorbet
3 cups superfine sugar
2 cups water
1¼ cups Perrier water
juice of 5 lemons
3 egg whites

For the caramelized Banyuls wine
3 cups Banyuls good quality French dessert wine

Pineapple gazpacho, mint granita, mixed red berries

For the gazpacho
2 medium-sized pineapples
8 cups water
1¾ cups granulated sugar
2 vanilla beans
finely grated zest of 1 lime

For the mint granita
2 cups water
1 cup sugar
bunch of fresh mint
½ cup Perrier water

To assemble and garnish
fresh red berry fruits
(raspberries, sliced
strawberries, wild
strawberries)
6 vanilla beans (optional)
slices of dried pineapple
frosted mint leaves (see note
at end of method)

For the gazpacho

Peel the pineapples, removing the hard core, and cut the flesh into fairly small pieces; place in a deep bowl. Bring the water to a boil with the sugar, vanilla beans and the grated lime zest. Pour this flavored sugar syrup all over the pineapple pieces and leave to stand, at cool room temperature, for 12 hours. After this time, drain the pineapple pieces (pour the syrup through a strainer and reserve) and reduce them to a smooth, thick liquid in the blender or food processor; strain through a fairly fine mesh strainer. Mix with sufficient syrup for a drinkable consistency. Chill in the refrigerator.

Mint granita

Bring the water and sugar to a boil, add the mint leaves and leave to infuse for 15 minutes. Strain through a fine mesh conical (*chinois*) strainer into a large pitcher or lipped mixing bowl; stir in the Perrier water. Pour into a rectangular, freezer-proof container or bowl and freeze until very firm but not rock hard.

To serve

Run the prongs of a fork firmly along the surface of the frozen mint granita, pressing hard and breaking it up into ice crystals. Mix these briefly and gently with the prepared berry fruits. Simply hull the raspberries and cultivated strawberries; the wild strawberries (*fraises des bois*) come away cleanly from their stalks when picked.

Spoon a heap of the granita and fruit mixture into the center of 6 deep soup plates and pour the pineapple gazpacho into the plate to surround it; alternatively, serve as shown on facing page.

Decorate with dried vanilla beans (optional), frosted mint leaves and slices of dried pineapple.

We love pineapple—and it shows! Here it makes an appearance as gazpacho, in a sweet version of the soup with lime juice, its ideal foil. The mint granita adds even more freshness. To frost mint leaves, select the best specimens, dip them one by one in stiffly beaten egg white and then dust with superfine sugar. Leave, uncovered, for up to 12 hours at room temperature. To keep these leaves crisp, store them in an airtight container. They will provide a handy decorative touch for a range of desserts.

Caramelized apricots, orange-flower water, almonds, orgeat milk sorbet

For the caramelized apricots
24 firm, fully ripe apricots
½ stick/2 oz unsalted butter
scant ½ cup superfine sugar
48 whole, blanched and peeled almonds
a few drops of pure almond essence
1 tbsp orange-flower water

For the orgeat milk sorbet
1½ cups orgeat syrup (orange ratafia)
3 cups light, pouring cream
1 cup whole milk

To assemble the dessert
coarsely chopped pistachio nuts
plain popcorn
a few fresh mint leaves

Orgeat milk sorbet

Mix the 3 ingredients in a pan and heat slowly until just below boiling point. Leave to cool, then freeze in a sorbetière or ice-cream maker. Place in the ice box of the refrigerator or in the freezer. (Orgeat syrup is available from certain delicatessens and good supermarkets; it is a mixture of orange-flower water, almond, milk and sugar.)

Caramelized apricots

Cut the apricots in half along their natural indentations and remove the pits. Heat the butter and sugar together in a very wide, heavy-bottomed skillet until very pale golden brown; add the apricots and cook them gently in the caramel, turning each half once. When they have heated through completely (but still hold their shape well), add the whole almonds and sprinkle in the almond essence and the orange-flower water. Stir very gently.

To assemble the dessert

Place 8 apricot halves with their flavored caramel liquid and 4 almonds in the center of 6 flat plates; add a scoop of orgeat milk sorbet. Decorate if wished with coarsely chopped pistachio nuts, plain popcorn and a few mint leaves.

Take care when turning the apricots as they heat through, barely cooking in the caramel, to avoid breaking them up at all or damaging their appearance. This dessert is the essence of Mediterranean flavor and delicacy; the better the apricots you use, the more successful the dish.

Strawberry fruit salad in its own syrup, vanilla mini-baba, vanilla ice cream

Strawberry syrup

Place the strawberries and sugar in the top of a double boiler over very gently simmering water and leave to heat through, rather than cook, for 45 minutes. A good deal of juice will be released, forming a light syrup; strain the strawberries in a nonmetallic fine mesh strainer. Do not press down on the fruit to extract more juice or the syrup will not be crystal clear. Allow to cool and then chill in the refrigerator.

Sweet yeast dough for the babas

Dissolve the fresh yeast or the dried yeast in 3 tablespoons of warm (not hot) milk and leave it to stand for 5 minutes while the yeast (re)activates. Mix the sifted flour, the dissolved yeast, ½ stick (2 oz) + 1 tbsp of the butter, salt and honey in the large bowl of a traditional food processor; attach the dough hook and process briefly; when homogeneous, add the eggs one by one, mixing in each egg thoroughly. The dough should be smooth and elastic and should leave the sides of the bowl cleanly; it should not be stiff. Leave to stand for 20 minutes.

Use the remaining butter to grease some little Savarin molds, dariole molds, or similar, small muffin pans. You will need at least 10 molds or pans. Break off pieces of the dough and place in the molds or pans (they should be less than two-thirds full at this point). Leave in a warm, draft-free place to rise for approximately 1 hour; when the dough has risen to fill the molds, it is ready to bake. Have the oven preheated to 350 °F. Bake the babas for approximately 15 minutes: they should be well risen and golden brown. Take them out of the oven, turn them out of their molds and leave to cool completely on a cake rack.

Soaking syrup for the babas

Bring the water and sugar to a boil. Slit the vanilla bean down its entire length and scrape out all the tiny, sticky seeds from inside with the sharp point of a knife; add these to the boiling syrup. Turn off the heat and leave to stand until completely cold. Dip the baba cakes in this syrup, immersing them completely to make sure they are soaked through.

Strawberry fruit salad

Rinse the strawberries briefly and hull them. Cut in half or in quarters, depending upon their size. Mix them gently with the shredded mint.

Assembling the dessert

Heap up the strawberries in mounds in fairly deep plates. Pour the strawberry syrup over them. On each plate place 2 syrup-soaked babas and a neatly rounded scoop of vanilla ice cream.

> Choose the most highly scented strawberries you can find, preferably freshly picked home grown or locally picked ones in season. Wild strawberries (*fraises des bois*) are probably the best but they are difficult to obtain outside Europe and their season is short. Do not refrigerate strawberries: this tends to make them lose their scent and flavor.

To serve 5

For the strawberry fruit salad
generous 1½ lb small, very fresh, ripe strawberries
1 small bunch fresh mint, snipped into thin strips

For the strawberry syrup
generous 1 lb very fresh, ripe strawberries
⅓ cup superfine sugar

For the sweet yeast baba dough
scant 1 oz fresh yeast or 2 tsp dried yeast
3 tbsp warm milk
1½ cups sifted white all-purpose flour
½ stick butter, softened at room temperature + 2 tbsp extra for greasing the molds
generous pinch of salt
scant 1 tsp clear, runny honey
5 whole eggs

For the vanilla syrup
2 cups water
⅔ cups sugar
1 vanilla bean

Serve with
2–3 cups best quality vanilla ice cream

Vanilla crème brulée, mascarpone ice cream, fresh strawberry juice

For the crème brulée
16 egg yolks
1¾ cups superfine sugar
2 cups whole milk
1 cup light, pouring cream
2 vanilla beans

For the fresh strawberry juice
2¼ lb very fresh, ripe strawberries
¾ cup superfine sugar

For the mascarpone ice cream
4 cups whole milk
10 egg yolks
1¼ cups superfine sugar
1½ cups Italian mascarpone
1 cup crème fraîche, preferably not very thick (see note at end of method)

For the topping
Cassonade (raw brown cane sugar)

Crème brulée

The day before you plan to serve this dessert, mix all the ingredients listed together (without heating any of them) as follows: beat the egg yolks with the superfine sugar until very pale; the mixture should form an unbroken ribbon when the whisk is lifted above it. Add the milk, cream, and the vanilla beans (having first slit them lengthwise and scraped the seeds out into the mixture). Chill in a cold larder or in the refrigerator, protected from any strong odors, to allow the vanilla to flavor and scent the mixture for 24 hours.

When this time has passed, preheat the oven to 195 °F. Pour the mixture through a very fine mesh strainer (a conical chinois if you have one) into a large pitcher and fill 10 porcelain ramekins up their inner grooves or "lips," just under ¼ inch below the rim. Cook in the oven for approximately 1 hour or until the custard mixture has set firmly. Allow to cool and then chill in the refrigerator.

Fresh strawberry juice

Place the prepared strawberries with the sugar in the top of a double boiler, over gently simmering water. Cover and heat for 45 minutes. Strain through a fine mesh non-metallic strainer; do not press down on the strawberries to extract extra liquid or the juice will be cloudy. Allow to cool and then chill in the refrigerator.

Mascarpone ice cream

Pour the milk into a large pan and slowly heat to just below boiling point. Beat the egg yolks and the sugar until very pale and fluffy (to the "ribbon" stage, see above). Gradually add the milk in a thin stream while beating continuously. Cook in a heavy-bottomed pan over a low heat or use a large double boiler and stir with a spatula as the custard gradually thickens. Do not allow to boil at any point. Remove from heat. Stir in the mascarpone, mixing well. Leave to stand until cold, stirring at intervals, then process in an ice-cream maker.

Make sure you take this ice cream out of the freezer 1 hour before serving it and leave it to stand at cool room temperature. Beat the crème fraîche until it is as frothy as a milk shake; it should not be stiff; fold it into the mascarpone ice cream just before serving.

Assembling the dessert

Sprinkle the cassonade (raw brown cane sugar) evenly over the surface of the chilled ramekins of custard and place them under a very hot broiler to caramelize just before serving. Suggested presentation: place a crème brulée on a square plate, place a ramekin of mascarpone ice cream beside it and stand a small, narrow tumbler or liqueur glass of the strawberry juice on the same plate.

> If crème fraîche is not readily available a very good homemade substitute can be made by mixing together 1 cup whipping cream and 2 tablespoons buttermilk in a glass bowl. Cover and leave to stand at room temperature for at least 8 hours, or up to 24 hours, until very thick. Stir well and refrigerate. It will keep for 7–10 days.

Crab and clam croquettes with fresh chile sauce

To serve 4

For the sauce
1 onion
1 garlic clove
1 tomato
1 lime
1 fresh chile pepper
scant ½ cup olive oil
juice of 1 lime
pinch of ground cumin
a few fennel seeds, lightly crushed
small bunch fresh cilantro
salt

For the croquettes
1 generous cup all-purpose flour
1 scant tbsp baking powder
½ cup whole milk
7 oz white crab meat
3½ oz fresh cherrystone shell clams (shelled weight) or drained canned clams
1 small onion, minced
2 large scallions
2 small garlic cloves, crushed
1 fresh chile pepper, minced
salt

For cooking and assembling the dish
4 cups peanut oil for frying
12 fresh cilantro leaves
wooden skewers or satay sticks (optional)
salt

The sauce

The day before you plan to serve this dish, prepare the sauce: peel and mince the onion; crush the garlic clove; blanch, peel, and seed the tomato, cut the flesh into small dice. Peel off all the pith, peel, and membrane from the lime, making it easy to extract the segments from the remaining membrane; cut these segments into small dice. Remove the remains of stalk and the seeds from the chile pepper and mince the rest. As you prepare all these ingredients, place them in a bowl and then add the remaining ingredients, except the fresh cilantro. Cover tightly and leave to stand overnight for the flavors to develop.

The croquettes

The next day, when it is time to prepare and cook the croquettes, sift the flour with the baking powder into a large bowl and mix with sufficient milk until you have a batter that is thicker than you would make for pancakes: it must be thick enough to bind all the additional ingredients you are about to add, and hold them together as they fry. Add the crab flesh, clams (use canned, well-drained small clams if necessary) and the remaining ingredients, adding the salt to taste. If the batter is not thick enough, stir in a very little additional sifted flour.

Cooking and serving

Heat the frying oil to 350 °F. Take a heaped coffee spoon of the crab mixture and push this little portion of mixture off the spoon with a fingertip, allowing it to fall into the hot oil. Do likewise with the remaining mixture, removing the croquettes from the oil with a slotted spoon when they are browned all over; finish draining them briefly on paper towels, sprinkle with a little salt and serve at once, accompanied by the chile sauce (to which the snipped fresh cilantro leaves should be added at the last minute). Decorate with the extra 12 cilantro leaves.

How do you choose which types of chile pepper to use? Shops specializing in Asian and Far Eastern vegetables usually stock a variety, in all sorts of shapes, sizes, and colors. We like to use the fresh Thai or Vietnamese red or green chiles, thin and elongated and ranging from 1½–2½ inches in length. To prepare these, slit them from top to bottom and remove the seeds with the tip of a small knife. Cut away any pale parts and remains of the stalk before mincing the chile. Don't touch your eyes or mouth while you are chopping chiles or immediately afterward! Wash your hands very thoroughly. Some cooks wear disposable gloves when preparing chiles...

Crunchy tuna-filled nori rolls, green papaya salad, sesame, watermelon, and wasabi sauce

For the tuna rolls
14 oz very fresh red tuna fillet
2 Japanese *nori* seaweed
sheets (see note at end of
recipe)
4 cups oil for frying
salt

**For the green papaya
salad**
1 large green papaya
3 tbsp best quality sesame
seed oil
1 tbsp rice wine vinegar
pinch of toasted sesame
seeds

**For the sesame,
watermelon, and wasabi
sauce**
1 large piece of fresh water
melon, seeds removed,
peeled
1 scant tsp commercially
prepared wasabi (see note at
end of recipe)

For the tempura batter
1 scant cup all-purpose flour
1 egg yolk
pinch of salt
½ cup iced water
2–3 small ice cubes

Tuna and nori rolls

Cut the tuna fillet into strips about 3 inches long, ¾ inch wide and ¾ inch thick. Cut out strips from the sheets of nori to the same length as the tuna pieces and wide enough to wrap around the tuna fillet, with a little extra for the overlap to secure the roll, leaving the tuna visible only at both ends. Roll up the tuna pieces tightly in the nori wrappers and press the two long edges over each other securely. Make 3 tuna rolls for each person. Place in the refrigerator.

Green papaya salad

Peel the papaya and scoop out all its seeds. Slice it very finely, using a mandoline or a julienne strip cutter. Cover with a damp cloth and chill in the refrigerator. Mix the sesame seed oil and the rice vinegar and dress the papaya with this, adding the pinch of sesame seeds; return the bowl to the refrigerator.

Watermelon and wasabi sauce

Extract the juice from the watermelon with a juicer and cook over a moderate heat until it has reduced to half its original volume and acquired a syrupy consistency. Stir in the spoonful of wasabi and chill in the refrigerator.

Tempura batter

Sift the flour into a large bowl, make a well in the middle and into it put the egg, salt, and iced water. Mix until the batter acquires the consistency of a fairly liquid pancake batter. Add the ice cubes.

Cooking and serving

Heat the oil to 350 °F ready for frying. Pop the tuna and *nori* rolls briefly one by one in the *tempura* batter, drain slightly and immediately add to the frying oil. When the batter turns a pale golden brown remove them from the oil; drain on paper towels and sprinkle with salt. Serve the tuna rolls on large flat plates with the green papaya salad and the watermelon and wasabi sauce, or use the presentation shown on the facing page.

This recipe has drawn on more than one source for its inspiration: Japan for the tempura; Thailand for the green papaya salad. Green papayas are usually available in good supermarkets, specialist greengrocers and in stores selling Far-Eastern foods. Choose a sound, firm, completely green fruit. *Nori* is made from dried reddish laver seaweed leaves and is normally used to wrap many varieties of sushi. Wasabi is a pale green horseradish relish, very hot on the tongue and highly flavored. It is available ready to use in tubes or as powder: all the latter needs is the addition of a few drops of water to form a thick paste and to be left for its distinctive aroma to develop. It is absolutely vital for the *tempura* batter to be kept icy cold until it is used if it is to have the delectable, airy crunchiness that makes it such a favorite.

Shrimp in tempura batter, fried plantains, sweet chile sauce

To serve 4

16 medium-sized shrimp, freshly peeled (see note in method)
oil for frying
salt

For the tempura batter
approximately ½ cup iced water
2 tbsp all-purpose flour
1 egg yolk
1 ice cube
salt

For the plantain fritters
2 ripe plantain bananas
4 cups peanut oil for frying
salt

For the sweet chile sauce
4 fresh red chile peppers
4 tbsp superfine sugar
juice of 1 lime
12 fresh cilantro leaves
salt

Tempura batter

Mix the iced water, flour, and salt. Beat in the egg yolk last of all. The resulting mixture should be a smooth batter that can be poured but is better described as a thick pancake batter. Chill the batter, having added the ice cube to it, to keep it very cold.

Sweet chile sauce

Slit the chile peppers in half (discarding the seeds) and blanch them briefly several times in boiling water, allowing them to cool between each immersion. Cut them into small pieces and place in a small pan with the sugar and ¾ cup water. Boil very gently indeed for as long as it takes for the contents of the pan to acquire a syrupy consistency. Leave to cool, then add the lime juice and the snipped or shredded cilantro leaves. Add a little salt.

Frying the shrimp in the tempura batter

Heat the frying oil to a temperature of 350 °F. Dip the shrimp in the batter and immediately add them to the hot oil; fry them until they are pale golden brown. As soon as they are ready, remove them with a slotted spoon and drain on paper towels. Sprinkle with a little salt, if wished. Keep hot.

Plantain fries

Peel the plantains and cut them into steak-fries-shaped pieces. Cook them in the very hot oil until they are crisp and golden brown (they take less time to cook than fries).
Finish draining on paper towels and sprinkle with salt.

To serve

Select an equal number of shrimp fried in tempura batter and plantain fries—one quarter of the total, and put these on each person's heated plate. Hand round the sauce separately, or serve in small individual bowls.

> Tempura batter must be icy cold and has to be fried in very hot oil: this is what gives it a delectable, delicate crispness and crunchiness. Choose ripe plantains, recognizable by their dark brown skins, blotched with black. If you can find only slightly under-ripe specimens, ripen them up in a warm kitchen for a few days.

Oyster tartare, passion fruit topping, brochettes of sole with gomashio

For the sole brochettes
1 very fresh, large sole fillet
4 wooden skewers or satay sticks
olive oil

For the gomashio
¾ cup toasted sesame seeds
very good quality sea salt
(*fleur de sel*, Maldon)

For the oyster tartare
8 absolutely fresh, live oysters, freshly opened and taken off the shell
scant 1 tsp of finely chopped chives
1 tomato, blanched, skinned, seeded and finely diced
(see method on p. 48)
1 tbsp olive oil

For the passion fruit sauce
2 large ripe passion fruits
2 tbsp fish stock
5 tbsp olive oil
salt, freshly ground white pepper

Sole brochettes

Slice the fillet of sole lengthwise into 4 strips of even width; thread each of these onto a satay stick or wooden skewer.

Gomashio

Mix the sesame seeds and the sea salt, crushing them together lightly (to release the seeds' flavor and help them adhere to the pieces of sole fillet).

Oyster tartare

Chop the oysters coarsely. Mix them in a bowl with the chives, diced tomato, and olive oil.

Passion fruit sauce

Cut each passion fruit in half and use a sharp-edged teaspoon to scrape out all the contents into a blender. Add the olive oil, the fish stock (this can be made with the trimmings from the sole; small plastic pots of fish fumet are also available in good delis and supermarkets), and some salt and freshly ground white pepper. Blend very thoroughly at high speed.

Cooking and assembling the dish

Heat a little olive oil in a wide nonstick skillet; cook the sole brochettes briefly over a high heat, turning them once or twice. Once they are cooked, roll them in the *gomashio* (have this ready spread out on a large plate). Choose 4 fairly large stemmed glasses or tumblers and into each spoon one-quarter of the oyster tartare, top with some passion fruit sauce and then place the sole brochette on top.

Gomashio is one of the simplest Japanese condiments to prepare: it consists of a mixture of toasted white sesame seeds and excellent sea salt. Buy the best sea salt you can afford for this seasoning, *fleur de sel* from the Atlantic coast of France, or Maldon from the North Sea coast of England are both rich in minerals and trace elements and go very well with the nutty sesame seed flavor. Passion fruit pulp has seeds in it that are tough but digestible; you may prefer to push the pulp through a fairly coarse-mesh strainer to get rid of them.

Salmon tataki, peanut sauce, crunchy asparagus spears

To serve 4

For the salmon *tataki*
14 oz salmon fillet, cut from
the center of the fish
2 tbsp olive oil

For the asparagus
16 large, green, very fresh
asparagus spears
4 cups oil for frying
tempura batter (see recipe on
p.128)
sea salt, table salt

**For the caramelized
balsamic vinegar**
2 cups balsamic vinegar

For the peanut sauce
scant ½ cup peanut butter
½ cup water
salt, freshly ground pepper

For the lemon vinaigrette
juice of ½ lemon
3 tbsp olive oil
salt, freshly ground pepper

For the gomashio
2 tbsp toasted sesame seeds
1 scant tsp best quality
sea salt

Salmon tataki

Slice the salmon fillet into 2 equal pieces. Heat the olive oil in a nonstick skillet, and when it is very hot sear the salmon pieces on both sides: they should be sealed on the surface, but not cooked inside. Refresh the pieces of salmon immediately by adding them to a bowl of iced water. When they are cold, place them on a clean cloth and dry them well. Place a large piece of plastic food wrap on the work surface. Place the first salmon piece flat on a piece of the food wrap and roll it up tightly, wrap and all, as if you were rolling up a Swiss roll. Secure both sides and tuck excess plastic wrap underneath the rolled up fish. Prepare the other piece of salmon in the same way. Chill in the refrigerator.

The asparagus

Peel, trim, and wash the asparagus; tie 12 spears into a neat bundle. Bring plenty of salted water to a boil in a large pan; cook the bundle of asparagus until tender but still crisp. Refresh the spears in a bowl of iced water, untie them and spread them out on paper towels to drain. Chill in the refrigerator.

Caramelized balsamic vinegar

Reduce the balsamic vinegar over a moderate heat in an uncovered, thick-based pan until it acquires a syrupy consistency. Care must be taken during the later stages or it may burn: if the syrup coats the bottom of the pan lightly when it is tipped to one side, it is ready.

Peanut sauce

Mix the water with the peanut butter. Season with salt and pepper and set aside.

Lemon vinaigrette

Mix all the ingredients.

Gomashio

Combine the sesame seeds with the sea salt. (See note on page 126.)

Frying the asparagus

Heat the oil for frying to 350 °F. Mix all the ingredients for the tempura batter. Dip the asparagus spears one by one in the batter and immediately add the batter-coated spears to the hot oil. Take them out when the batter is crisp and pale golden in color. Finish draining on paper towels and sprinkle with a little salt.

Assembling and serving the dish

Peel the remaining 4 asparagus spears and slice them into long, very thin strips using a mandoline or a very sharp knife. Dress them with the lemon vinaigrette.
Take the salmon rolls out of the refrigerator: cut them into neat slices and carefully remove the wrap from each slice.
Arrange 3 batter-coated asparagus spears on each plate, cover these with slices of the salmon *tataki* and sprinkle with *gomashio*. Top with some of the raw, finely sliced asparagus. Surround with the peanut sauce and a trickle of caramelized balsamic vinegar.

> To make a success out of this version of a Japanese dish, traditionally prepared with fillet of beef, choose only the freshest and best wild salmon (or very fresh tuna) and the freshest asparagus. Remember to have the tempura batter icy cold to make sure that it is very crisp and tender when cooked.

Crisp lobster spring rolls with avocado, tomato, and cilantro salsa

Lobster spring rolls

Add all the ingredients listed for the court-bouillon to 6 cups water. Bring to a boil and continue boiling for 10 minutes, then plunge the lobsters into the pan, allowing them to cook for only 3–4 minutes, depending on their size. Remove and plunge them immediately into a large bowl of iced water. Cut them lengthwise in half along the middle of their backs with a sharp, heavy knife and remove their tails from the shells. Extract all the meat from the claws and large front "legs." Cut each piece of the tail meat into 4 or 5 large pieces. Set aside with the claw meat.

Cut the spring roll wrappers into rectangles measuring 3 x 1½ inches; cut out as many rectangles as you have pieces of lobster to wrap. Spread the spring roll pieces out on the work surface. On each one place the following: 1 tomato "petal," a pinch of chives, 1 piece of lobster, then season with salt and pepper and roll up just as you would for a spring roll; secure the one free flap to the roll by threading a toothpick through them both, to keep each spring roll closed when it is fried.

Avocado, tomato, and cilantro salsa

Slice the avocados in half, removing their pits; scoop out the flesh into a bowl and mash it well with a fork, adding the lime juice, chopped scallion, and a little salt. Prepare the tomatoes: blanch for a few seconds in boiling water, refresh in cold water at once, peel and quarter them; take out all the central sections and the seeds, leaving only 4 "petal"-shaped pieces of their outer flesh. Cut these into little dice and add to the avocado mixture. Discard the seeds from the fresh chiles, chop the red flesh and stir into the salsa. Add the cilantro and a little more salt.

Cooking and serving

Heat the oil for frying to a temperature of 350 °F. Fry the lobster spring rolls for a few minutes, until they are crisp and golden brown; finish draining them on paper towels. Wrap the lobster spring rolls in small cloth or paper napkinds and place on the individual plates, with some of the avocado and chile salsa in a small bowl beside them. The crunchy spring rolls are dipped into the fresh yet peppery salsa before taking a bite.

> This avocado salsa is a version of Mexican guacamole, at one and the same time a sauce and a salad which is deliciously refreshing. In common with traditional guacamole, the salsa should not be too smooth. Cut the avocados in half, working around the central pit, twist to separate the two halves and use the point of the knife (carefully!) to spear the pit and remove it. Using a fork, crush the flesh while it is still in the skin (some avocado skins are too thin for this treatment) and then scoop all the flesh into a bowl. Prepared this way, the flesh still has some texture to it and is more interesting that way. Get rid of the chile seeds unless you like extremely fiery tastes—and always wash your hands thoroughly before touching your eyes when you have chopped or touched chiles.

To serve 4

**For the lobster
spring rolls**
4 lobsters, each weighing
approximately 1 lb
10 spring roll wrappers
(see note on p. 162)
32 slow-baked tomato
"petals" (see recipe on p. 60)
1 bunch of chives, finely
snipped or chopped
4 cups oil for frying
1 packet of wooden
toothpicks
salt, freshly ground pepper

For the court-bouillon
1 carrot, sliced into rounds
1 onion, sliced
green section of 1 leek, sliced
1 celery stalk, sliced
1 bouquet garni: 1 bay leaf,
sprig of fresh thyme
sea salt

For the avocado salsa
4 ripe avocados
1 large scallion or 1 fresh
mild white onion
juice of 1 lime
2 bright red, ripe tomatoes
2 fresh red chiles
leaves from a small bunch of
fresh cilantro, snipped or
coarsely chopped
salt

fish and seafood

Grilled langoustine tails with Thai red curry, braised bok choy, coconut milk soup

For the langoustines with red curry
4 large, very fresh raw langoustines (Dublin Bay prawns)
1 tbsp Thai red curry paste (see note at end of method)
1 tbsp olive oil
4 bamboo satay sticks
salt

For the braised bok choy
4 heads of bok choy (see note on p. 22)
1½ tbsp butter
1 large scallion or fresh, mild white onion, thinly sliced
salt, freshly ground pepper

For the coconut milk soup
1 shallot, peeled and very thinly sliced
1 tbsp olive oil
1 inch length of fresh galangal root, peeled
1 inch piece of fresh ginger, peeled
small can of coconut milk, unsweetened
juice of ½ lime
a few fresh cilantro leaves
salt

For the fried apple relish
2 Granny Smith apples
½ tbsp butter
salt, freshly ground pepper

Langoustines with Thai red curry paste

Peel the langoustines (see note on page 83) after you have removed their heads, leaving the tail flippers intact and attached. Reserve the heads and shells for the stock. Impale each langoustine tail on a bamboo satay stick.

Mix the Thai red curry paste with a very little water and the olive oil; spoon this all over the langoustines on their sticks and leave them in a cool place to soak up the flavors for 1 hour. Place the heads and shells of the langoustines in a pan, add enough water to cover them and boil over a moderate heat for 20 minutes, then strain the stock into a jug through a fine mesh strainer pressing down hard to extract the juice and flavor. Return to the pan and boil gently until reduced to half its original volume. Set aside.

Braised bok choy

Trim the bok choy, wash well, and cut each separate stem and its leaf into wide strips. Heat the butter in a thick-based pan, fry the bok choy and the scallion over a moderate heat; add a little water and simmer for 10 minutes. Season to taste and keep hot.

Coconut milk soup

Cook the shallot over a very gentle heat in the olive oil; when it is soft, add the langoustine stock, the galangal, and the ginger. Simmer over a low heat for 15 minutes to enable the galangal and ginger to flavor the mixture. Do not allow to boil once you have added the coconut milk, together with the lime juice. Taste and add more seasoning if wished. Remove from the heat and add the cilantro leaves at the last minute.

Apple relish

Cut the apples into very thin slices, then cut across these in turn, to produce little matchstick pieces (julienne strips). Fry these in a very little butter over a high heat very briefly; the apple strips should retain some of their crispness. Season with salt and pepper.

Cooking and presentation

Fry the langoustines very briefly in a nonstick skillet over a high heat; they taste much better if they are slightly undercooked. Sprinkle with a little salt.

Allocate 3 little serving pots for each person: one for the langoustine-flavored coconut soup; one for the apple relish and one for the braised bok choy. Stand them on large plates with a curried langoustine brochette on each.

> Thai red curry paste is very widely sold nowadays, no longer confined to Far-Eastern specialist food shops. It is very hot, with plenty of chiles, so you may choose to taste it before using some for the first time.

Adventures in faraway places:
The French East Indies Company

La Compagnie Française des Indes Orientales (The French East Indies Company) was our main source of inspiration when planning the first Compagnie des Comptoirs. Memories of this seafaring enterprise are evoked by the soft patina of tropical woods, nautical charts on the walls, and the subtle impression of setting out on a voyage. The old, four-leaved Afghan door is no mere entrance; it marks the threshold of a world where we can realize our dreams.

It begins with a poetic succession of names: Yanam, Mahe, Pondicherry, Karikal, Chandernagore, Surat—the French trading posts in India. These can be accompanied, in their sheer musicality, by the names Goa, Cochin, Calicut; other trading posts that were originally Portuguese but that

Above: a multicolored array of vegetables arranged with great care, in a market in south India.
Facing page, left: the antique Afghan door leading into La Compagnie des Comptoirs in Montpellier.

Below: *the market in Pondicherry in 1907; the beautiful and brilliant colors, the cacophony of different languages and dialects and the intoxicating wafts of scent from flowers, fruits, and spices are all left to the imagination.*
Facing page, right: *cinnamon sticks: rolled-up pieces of bark from the cinnamon tree.*

became Dutch. Spices were sought after not only as aromatics and flavorings but also for their anti-septic and preservative properties. Cardamom, galangal, ginger, nutmeg, long pepper, chile pepper and other varieties of capsicum, cinnamon, fenugreek, cloves, turmeric, saffron, and above all black pepper: this coveted merchandise excited fierce competition and even caused wars. The history of the trading posts was essentially a race for the largest possible share in the spice trade.

The spice race

The Portuguese and Spanish founded the first colonial trading posts in the late 1400s. From 1588 on, however, they lost power to the Dutch. The VOM (*Verenigde Oost-Indische Maatschappij*, United East India Company), established in 1602, was effectively a state unto itself: it could mint coin, raise an army, declare war, negotiate treaties, and, of course, trade in spices, ivory, and silks, which it bought at low prices and sold on at a margin of up to 500 percent. While England had founded the East India Company in 1600, it was not until 1664 that Colbert formed the Compagnie Française des Indes Orientales; once both these countries had become involved, however, it was not long before more confrontations in a long and hard contest followed.

The activities of the French company concentrated on the islands of the Indian Ocean and India, its ships trading between the Indian port of Surat and the French ports of Lorient, Bordeaux, Nantes, and La Rochelle, as well as the arsenal of Rochefort. Pondicherry, the headquarters of the French trading activities in India, was founded in 1674 on the Coromandel coast (now Tamil Nadu); Chandernagore, in Bengal, on the Ganges delta, followed in 1676. The pepper trade was plied along the Kerala and Malabar coasts, while cinnamon was traded in Sri Lanka, and the cassia, star anise, and galangal trade centered on China. In the Maldives, French traders acquired cowry shells that served as currency in Africa for the purchase of slaves. Slaves were exchanged in the West Indies for cane sugar and rum, which were bartered to buy more slaves, spices, precious stones, and silks.

The taste of India—and a taste for India

During the eighteenth century new trading posts were founded: Mahe in Kerala; Yanam in Andhra Pradesh, and Karikal in Tamil Nadu. France took possession of more territory and set up protectorates. Treaties were signed with the rajahs: the colonial governors employed Indian personnel who maintained good relations with the princely states' rulers through their courtiers. As was later the case with the British Raj, the colonists developed a taste for the spicy flavors of Indian foods (it was the English who invented curry powder, hitherto unknown in India). The colonists also attended Indian festive events. Marriage between the races became widespread. In 1790, when the French company's activities came to an end, only two wholly French families remained.

Farther to the south and in the West Indies (the Caribbean), cultivation of tropical crops was developed. The Ile Bourbon and the Ile de France (now Réunion and Mauritius) produced vanilla and sugar. Meanwhile the Dutch and the English sought every means to destroy French trading posts and to thwart their activities, which at one point involved a blockade of the mouth of the Ganges. Increasingly, commercial activity was forced to shift to the West Indies, with its increasingly important trade in sugar, rum, coffee, chocolate, and slaves. France's participation in the East Indies' trade declined; in 1763, with the signature of the Treaty of Paris, France ceded to England all her Indian possessions with the exception of only five trading posts. The French Company of the East Indies was to last only another twenty-seven years, although the Comptoirs (trading posts) remained French territories until 1954.

In that year, as the French administrators departed, the new mayor of Chandernagore expressed some nostalgia as he bade them farewell, a fairly rare sentiment in the history of decolonization: "In the secular history of our two nations, one modern, the other ancient, a new chapter begins… which will no longer be polluted by bitter and rancorous relationships between governors and the governed, a chapter that will grow happier with each passing day because of the kindly and cordial relationships that now exist between our two friendly nations."

Above: *a spice box.* Facing page, left: *turmeric rhizomes, more bitter than saffron but even more highly colored. Turmeric is used in many curries; the most sought-after variety comes from Bengal.*

137

Adventures in faraway places: The French East Indies

Clam soup with coconut milk, fresh galangal and turmeric, chorizo

4½–4¾ lb fresh clams in their shells
1 shallot, minced
scant ½ oz fresh ginger
scant 1 oz fresh galangal
1 tbsp fresh turmeric or generous pinch turmeric powder
½ small chile pepper
2 blanched, peeled, seeded tomatoes (see method on p. 48)
olive oil
¾ cup coconut milk (canned, unsweetened)

To serve

small bunch fresh cilantro
1 chorizo sausage (good quality, Spanish)
juice of 1 lime
olive oil
salt, freshly ground pepper

Wash the clams extremely well in several changes of cold, fresh water; discard any that do not close when handled; drain them and set aside.

Mince the peeled shallot; peel the ginger and grate it finely. Peel the galangal and cut it into wafer-thin slices. Peel and mince the fresh turmeric, if used. Remove the seeds from the chile pepper. Snip the cilantro leaves and set aside for garnishing the finished dish.

Heat 1 tablespoon of olive oil in a wide, deep, heavy-bottomed pan or fireproof/oven-to-table casserole dish and cook the shallot gently without allowing it to brown at all; add the ginger, galangal, and turmeric. Add all the clams, cover and cook over a moderate heat until they have all opened (this will only take a few minutes); discard any clams that do not open.

Use a slotted ladle to take the clams out of the pan; keep them warm. Increase the heat under the cooking juices and clam juice left behind in the pan and add the roughly chopped tomatoes. Cook, uncovered, until the liquid has reduced to half its original volume, add as much of the chile as you wish, and finish by pouring in the coconut milk. Simmer for a few minutes.

Serving

Cut 20 very thin slices from the chorizo sausage. Fry them briefly in a nonstick skillet over a high heat and drain on paper towels. Return the clams to the sauce in the large pan, sprinkle the chopped cilantro all over them, followed by the lime juice. Add more seasoning if wished and add the thin slices of fried chorizo last of all. Drizzle a little olive oil around the clams and serve at once. Season to taste.

The association of seafood (clams) with pork (chorizo) owes much to the influence of Spain's culinary tradition and, with the use of cilantro, to Portuguese cooking. Use only the very best, moist chorizo, which will have a wonderful, subtle taste and aroma. The coconut milk has nothing to do with the Iberian peninsula, but its mildness and velvety texture contribute to the success of this highly flavored dish.

Gurnard fillet baked in a banana leaf, eggplant and mango, spicy tomato sauce

To serve 4

For the fish parcels
600 g (1¼ lb) gurnard fillets,
or red snapper (see note at
end of method)
2 fresh, green banana leaves
4 tbsp olive oil
salt, freshly ground pepper
wooden toothpicks

**For the eggplant and
mango compote**
1 eggplant
1 ripe but firm mango
1 tbsp olive oil
salt, freshly ground pepper

**For the spicy, syrupy
tomato sauce**
14 oz very ripe tomatoes
¾ cup unrefined superfine
sugar
1 tbsp tomato paste
a dash of sherry vinegar
½ fresh chile pepper
(optional)
2 tbsp olive oil
salt, freshly ground pepper

Eggplant and mango compote

Peel the mango and the eggplant and cut both into large dice. Heat the eggplant and the mango in the olive oil in a pan over a gentle heat; cover and cook very slowly until they are very soft. Remove the lid. If there is any excess moisture left in the pan, cook until it has evaporated completely. Season with salt and pepper.

Fish parcels

Cut the cleaned and prepared fillets into 4 portions. Heat the banana leaves by holding them some way above a gas burner and move them around to heat evenly; this will soften them. Cut out 4 pieces, each into an 8-inch square. Spoon a generous tablespoon of the eggplant and mango compote onto the middle of the lower half of each banana leaf square. Place a fish fillet on top of this, sprinkle with a tablespoonful of olive oil and season with salt and pepper.

Fold over the upper half of each square, enclosing the fish and compote, and secure with several toothpicks to make a neat parcel. Preheat the oven to 350 °F.

Spicy tomato sauce

Blanch the tomatoes for a few second in boiling water, peel them, remove the seeds, and then chop them roughly. Place the tomatoes and all the other ingredients listed for the sauce in a thick-bottomed pan and bring to a boil. Turn down the heat and simmer very gently for 1½ hours. Remove from the heat; purée in the blender and add seasoning if needed. Set aside.

Cooking and assembling the dish

Bake the fish parcels in the oven for 15–20 minutes, depending on the thickness of the fish fillets. Remove the toothpicks and serve, using the banana leaves as plates (on top of ordinary plates), handing round the spiced tomato sauce.

Gurnard (*Trigla lucerna*, also known as the tub gurnard or tub-fish) is caught off the Mediterranean coastline and is remarkable for its beautiful coloration (rosy red on its back, pectoral fins patterned with blue and green) and for its delicate taste. It is an important ingredient in *bouillabaisse*. Red snapper is a good substitute.

Fillet of sea bass with lemon grass, stir-fried vegetables, tapioca and ginger

For the sea bass fillets

1½ lb sea bass fillets, scaled
but not skinned
4 fresh lemon grass stalks
olive oil

**For the tapioca and
ginger sauce**

4 cups milk
scant ½ oz tapioca
2 oz *perles du Japon*
2½ tbsp peeled, finely grated
fresh ginger
1 tsp olive oil
salt, freshly ground pepper

For the vegetables

2 tbsp grapeseed oil
1 small Chinese cabbage
(Chinese leaves), finely sliced
2 heads of bok choy (see note
on p. 28) cut into large slices
5 oz shiitake mushrooms
2 carrots, sliced into very
thin rounds
2 mild onions, very
finely sliced
2½ tbsp fresh ginger, peeled
and minced
1 garlic clove, crushed
small bunch of fresh cilantro
salt, freshly ground pepper

Last-minute seasoning

best quality sea salt, freshly
ground Sichuan peppercorns

Sea bass fillets

Cut the sea bass fillets into 4 equal portions, weighing approximately 5 oz each.

Strip off the outermost layers of the lemon grass and trim the remaining stalk to an equal length and thickness (longer than the fish fillets). Slice each stalk in half, cutting at a very oblique angle to make the cut surface sharp: thread the sharp, newly cut ends diagonally through the fillets, 2 for each fillet (they will cross each other in the center of the fillet, see facing page).

Tapioca and ginger sauce

Bring the milk to a boil in a heavy-bottomed pan; stir in the rest of the ingredients listed under this heading, except the seasoning. Simmer very gently without allowing to boil (approximately 175 °F is the ideal temperature) for 45 minutes, then season with salt and pepper. Set aside and keep warm.

Stir-fried vegetables

Heat the grapeseed oil over a high heat in a wok. Add all the prepared vegetables and stir-fry them until they are just tender but still very crisp; season with salt and pepper to taste, remove from the heat and add the cilantro leaves.

Cooking the fish and assembling the dish

Heat a very little olive oil in a large, nonstick skillet over a high heat. Place the fillets in the pan, skin side down. Do not turn the fillets until the skin is crisp and brown; cook for about 1 minute after turning. Set aside. Arrange a portion of the stir-fried vegetables in the center of each plate, place the sea bass fillet on top of them, skin side uppermost, sprinkle with a little sea salt (*fleur de sel* or Maldon) and give a couple of twists of the peppermill to sprinkle with Sichuan pepper. Surround with the *perles du Japon* and tapioca sauce, flavored with ginger.

> This recipe provides an original way of using tapioca and *perles du Japon*, tender and translucent cereal ingredients that seem to be making a welcome return after years of neglect. You will need to search for the *perles de Japon*, but they are still manufactured in Nantes in France and a specialist store or delicatessen may stock them. A tip: ginger is easily peeled by rubbing the sharp edge of a teaspoon against the skin!

Giant shrimp, fruit grilled à la plancha, cashew nut and tomato salsa

For the fruits *à la plancha*
1 small pineapple
1 cantaloupe melon
(muskmelon)
2 mangoes (ripe but firm)
1 tbsp olive oil
salt, freshly ground pepper

For the marinated shrimp
8 very large fresh shrimp or
8 frozen shrimp (thawed)
olive oil
2 tbsp fresh ginger, peeled
and crushed
½ chile pepper, seeded
and minced
juice of ½ lime
Sichuan peppercorns

For the cashew nut and tomato salsa
juice of 1 lime
1 cup olive oil
2 blanched, peeled, seeded
tomatoes, finely diced
small bunch fresh cilantro,
finely snipped or coarsely
chopped
½ cup cashew nuts, toasted
and coarsely chopped
salt, freshly ground pepper

Peel the pineapple, remove the tough, central core and cut the flesh into slices ½ inch thick. Cut the melon into fairly small sections (see facing page), remove the seeds but do not peel. Do not peel the mangoes; cut the flesh into slices ½ inch thick, slicing them away from the pit as neatly as possible.

Peel the shrimp but leave their heads and tail flippers attached. Marinate them in a cool place in a mixture of 2 tablespoons olive oil, the crushed ginger, and the minced fresh chile.

Cashew nut and tomato salsa

Mix the lime juice with a little table salt and a twist of freshly ground pepper. Add the diced tomatoes (see preparation method on page 54), the cilantro leaves and the chopped cashew nuts; mix well.

Grilled fruits *à la plancha*

Cook the prepared fruit on a griddle, or in a ridged nonstick griddle pan with a very little olive oil. Season with salt and pepper when seared and lightly cooked.

Cooking the shrimp

Heat a little olive oil in a large, nonstick skillet over a high heat and fry the shrimp briefly, turning them once. When they are cooked, sprinkle them with a little lime juice and some freshly ground Sichuan pepper.

To serve

Arrange a selection of the fruit attractively in the center of each plate, add 2 shrimp and surround with some of the cashew nut and tomato salsa.

Grilling *à la plancha* is an original and delicious way of preparing fruit as one of the constituents of a savory dish. Cashew nuts are all too often confined to the salted variety, served with drinks. When crushed they are used to thicken and add interest to curries, and to Southeast Asian and Brazilian sauces. In this recipe they add a crunchy texture to the subtly sweet-sour taste of the finished dish.

Belly of pork with allspice, polenta, compote of onions and figs

For the pork belly with allspice
4 pieces of best belly of pork for grilling, each weighing 8 oz
generous pinch of ground allspice
juice of 1 lime
2 tbsp olive oil (+ 3 extra tbsp for cooking and serving)
best quality sea salt, freshly ground pepper

For the polenta
2 cups milk
3 tbsp unsalted butter
¾ cup course-grain polenta
3 tbsp mascarpone

For the compote of onions and figs
4 presoftened, large dried figs
4 mild white onions
¼ stick/1 oz unsalted butter
pinch of superfine sugar
⅓ cup sherry vinegar
2 tbsp olive oil
2 tbsp soy sauce
¾ cup chicken stock or water (as needed)
salt, freshly ground pepper

Place the pieces of pork belly in a shallow dish and rub the allspice powder well into them; do the same with the lime juice and then with the olive oil. Leave to stand for 30 minutes in a cool place.

Polenta
Pour the milk into a thick-bottomed pan, add the butter (cut into small pieces) and bring to a boil. Sprinkle in the polenta while stirring continuously and energetically with a balloon whisk; continue cooking over a gentle heat for 30 minutes. Stir in the mascarpone when the polenta is cooked and keep it hot.

Compote of onions and figs
Slice the figs thinly; peel and trim the onions and cut them into wafer-thin slices. Place a heavy-bottomed pan over a low heat, add the butter, followed by the figs and onions. Sprinkle with the sugar, cover, and cook gently without allowing the onions to brown at all. When the juice or moisture from the onions has almost completely evaporated, stir in one-third of the sherry vinegar, scraping the bottom of the pan with a wooden spatula, and continue cooking, uncovered, until the vinegar has totally evaporated. Repeat this process twice, with the remaining two-thirds of the vinegar. Remove from the heat. Transfer the contents of the pan to a food processor or large blender, add the olive oil and soy sauce, and process until very smooth. Add a little chicken stock or water if the mixture is too thick. Add seasoning to taste; transfer to a dish and keep hot.

Pork belly with allspice
Heat 1 tbsp olive oil in a very wide, nonstick skillet and fry the pieces of pork belly over a moderate heat for approximately 20 minutes; at the end of this time they should be cooked through and browned on both sides. Sprinkle the pork with sea salt and freshly ground pepper.

Serving the dish
On each heated plate, place a large, well-rounded spoonful of polenta; press down lightly in the center of this mound with a tablespoon and fill the resulting hollow with onion and fig compote. Place each person's portion of pork belly beside the polenta and surround with a trace of olive oil.

> If you are short of time, you can use quick-cooking polenta or even the pre-cooked polenta sold in airtight plastic wrapping; the latter will be much heavier and less fluffy than home-cooked polenta, which should nevertheless be thick enough to hold its shape when spooned onto the plates. The belly of pork must be very well cooked and it should not be hurried over too high a heat; allow more time if necessary and check at frequent intervals.

Duck roasted on the bone, spiced date chutney, fluffy oat cakes, wine and passion fruit sauce

To serve 4

2 ducks (minus their legs and wings)
salt, freshly ground pepper

For the date chutney
7 oz dates
1 mild onion
¼ stick/1 oz butter
generous pinch allspice
1 tbsp superfine sugar
3½ tbsp vinegar
salt, freshly ground pepper

For the fluffy oat cakes
2½ cups hot milk
1½ sticks/6 oz butter
1⅓ cups rolled oats
6 eggs
salt, freshly ground pepper

For the sauce
3½ oz shallots, minced
1 stick/4 oz butter
2 cups very good, non-vintage dry red wine
1 cup passion fruit purée (see note at end of method)
2 cups rich duck stock (see note at end of method)
4 tbsp superfine sugar
salt, freshly ground pepper

Spiced date chutney

Take the pits out of the dates and cut the flesh into small pieces. Chop the onion and cook it in the butter over a gentle heat until it is transparent. Add the dates, followed by salt, pepper, the allspice, and the sugar. Cook for a minute or two and then add the vinegar, stirring well. Allow to cook over a low heat until the mixture has thickened to a suitable consistency for chutney. Set aside.

Passion fruit and wine sauce

Cook the shallots very gently in the butter. When they are transparent, add the red wine and boil gently, uncovered, until nearly all the wine has evaporated. Stir in the passion fruit purée, the rich duck stock, and the sugar. Boil gently, uncovered, to reduce until the sauce is syrupy and has thickened slightly. Add the butter, cut into pieces, and whisk these into the sauce as they melt. Use a hand-held electric beater to homogenize the sauce and add seasoning to taste.

Fluffy oat cakes

Preheat the oven to 350 °F.
Heat the milk with the butter until very hot but not quite boiling and stir in the rolled oats. Leave to stand for 20–25 minutes. Separate the egg yolks from the whites; stir the yolks into the oats. Whisk the egg whites stiffly and combine them gently with the oat mixture. Season with salt and pepper.
Spoon the oat mixture into nonstick dariole molds, filling them two-thirds full. Bake in the oven until well risen and firm to the touch. Remove from the oven and increase the temperature to 425 °F.

Cooking the duck and serving

Roast the duck bodies (i.e. minus their legs and wings) in a large, heavy-bottomed fireproof casserole dish, allowing them to cook all over for sufficient time to brown and crisp the skin; the fat underneath the skin should start to melt. When the skin is crisp, turn the ducks so that the breasts are uppermost, return the dish to the oven and continue roasting for 10 minutes. When the ducks are done, take them out of the oven and leave to stand in a warm place for 5–10 minutes before carving. Season with salt and pepper. Carve into long, fairly thick slices. Place on each heated plate a fluffy oat cake, a spoonful of date chutney, and slices of duck breast. Surround with the passion fruit sauce and, if wished, a trickle of very good olive oil.

> To make your own rich duck stock, make sure you are given the duck giblets with the birds themselves. Trim the livers, hearts, and necks of any fat or discoloration and chop them very coarsely. Fry them gently in a little butter with some sliced carrot and onion until lightly browned. Add 3 cups of water and some salt and pepper. Bring to a boil, then simmer gently, uncovered, for 1 hour. Pour this stock through a fine-mesh strainer and use it to make the sauce. To save time and trouble, thick passion fruit purée is sometimes available deep-frozen; make sure it is not sweetened. Otherwise follow the method given on p. 126 to prepare unsweetened purée of fresh passion fruits.

Chicken satay with two sauces, coconut-flavored rice parcels

For the chicken satay
1 generous cup ground chicken
peanut oil
fresh turmeric
fresh galangal
1 fresh lemon grass stalk
1 garlic clove, crushed
1 scant tbsp fresh ginger, peeled and grated
½ fresh chile, chopped
scant 1 oz jaggery (see note after method)
juice of ½ lime
2 shallots, sliced and fried

For the satay (peanut) sauce
fresh lemon grass stalk
fresh ginger
1½ cups toasted peanuts
2 oz tamarind paste
juice of ½ lime
2 oz hot shrimp paste
2 garlic cloves, finely chopped
fresh chile, minced
1 cup soy bean oil

For the pineapple sauce
2½ oz tamarind paste
2 cups fresh pineapple juice
2 oz hot shrimp paste
2 shallots, minced
2 garlic cloves, minced
⅛ fresh chile, minced
1 cup soy bean oil

For the rice
¾ cup Thai rice
½ cup canned coconut milk
1 banana leaf

Chicken satay mixture

Chop sufficient fresh turmeric and galangal to yield 1 tablespoon of each. Finely chop the lemon grass. Mix all the ingredients listed for the chicken mixture until homogeneous. Add more seasoning if wished. Take some of the chicken mixture and press it around the satay stick, shaping it into a flattened ball covering about a quarter of each stick.

Two sauces

Satay (peanut) sauce: crush the toasted peanuts; finely chop sufficient lemon grass to yield 2 tablespoonfuls and sufficient ginger to yield 1 tablespoonful. The next stage is similar for both sauces. Dilute the tamarind paste for the pineapple sauce by placing it in a fine-mesh plastic strainer and lower it halfway into a bowl of pineapple juice; stir the tamarind in the strainer with a small wooden spoon until it has completely dissolved. Follow the same procedure with more tamarind paste for the satay sauce but use a fairly small bowl containing the lime juice diluted with cold water. Stir the shrimp paste into these bowls of tamarind solution; add all the remaining ingredients. Stir table salt according to taste into the sauces. Set aside the two bowls.

Coconut-flavored rice parcels

Add sufficient cold water to the rice to cover it by ⅜ inch. Bring to a boil, cover tightly and cook over a very gentle heat until all the water has been absorbed by the rice, which should be tender but still have a little "bite" left in the grains. Add the coconut milk, cover tightly again, and return to a very gentle heat for 2 minutes; remove from the heat and leave to stand for 10 minutes. Spread the rice out in an even layer in a wide, shallow dish; when cold, add salt to taste and press down again into an even layer.

Heat the banana leaf over a gas burner to soften it. Cut out 4 large squares. Use a palette knife to mark out 4 squares of rice about half the size of the banana leaf squares; lift these "cakes" of rice onto the banana leaf squares and wrap them up, securing with toothpicks.

Cooking the satay sticks and serving

Preheat the oven to 325 °F.

Heat a little peanut oil in a very wide skillet and fry the satay sticks flat, turning once. Keep hot. Meanwhile reheat the rice packets in the oven. Serve them on plates, together with two small bowls, each containing a little of the two dipping sauces. The satay sticks can be served on the same plate or put into a tumbler, with a wedge of lime if wished.

Jaggery or palm sugar is sold in shops that specialize in Southeast-Asian foods, usually in the form of large cakes of unrefined sugar that have to be broken into pieces with a mallet. Asian grocery stores or the larger supermarkets will usually have all the other ingredients, such as tamarind paste, hot shrimp paste, coconut milk, Thai rice, galangal, fresh chiles, and fresh turmeric (you can substitute scant 1 teaspoon of turmeric powder for this last ingredient). Banana leaves may prove something of a challenge: try Latin markets.

Veal chops marinated "à l'orientale" with a chinoiserie of linguine and vegetables

To serve 4

4 veal chops, each
weighing 8–9 oz
4 oz fresh linguine pasta
olive oil
salt, freshly ground pepper

For the marinade
juice of 1 lime
scant ½ cup soy sauce
scant 1 tsp of clear, runny
honey
small piece of fresh ginger,
peeled and grated
2 tbsp sesame seed oil
½ garlic clove, crushed

**For the mixed julienne
strips of vegetables**
1 carrot
4 oz soy bean sprouts
1 leek
¼ Chinese cabbage
(Chinese leaves)
12 fresh shiitake mushrooms
2 large scallions or fresh
white onions, cut into strips
or sliced into thin rings
small bunch fresh cilantro
sesame seed oil
soy sauce
salt, freshly ground pepper

To serve
generous pinch of toasted
sesame seeds

Start preparing this dish a day in advance: mix all the marinade ingredients and marinate the veal chops in a cool place or refrigerator.

The linguine pasta

Shortly before you plan to serve this dish, bring a large pan of salted water to a boil, add scant 1 teaspoon of olive oil and cook the linguine until they are just tender but still have a little bite left in them (al dente). Drain and rinse under the cold faucet. Drain again.

Julienne of vegetables for the "chinoiserie"

Peel and trim the vegetables and cut them all into julienne strips except the bean sprouts; leave those as they are except for discarding as many of the bitter little green seed pods as possible.

Cooking the veal chops

Take the chops out of the marinade and wipe them dry with paper towels. Pour ½ cup of the marinade into a small pan and reduce over a gentle heat. Add seasoning if necessary and keep warm.

Fry the chops over a moderate heat, turning them once: they should be lightly browned on the outside, still slightly pink inside. Wrap them in foil and keep warm.

Cooking the vegetables

Heat a little sesame seed oil in a wok or large, nonstick skillet and stir-fry all the vegetables over a fairly high heat, starting with the carrots: cook these for 1 minute, then add the shiitake mushrooms; stir-fry these for 1 minute, then at 1-minute intervals add the leek, followed by the Chinese cabbage, the scallions, and finally the bean sprouts. Add the cilantro leaves, remove from the heat immediately and sprinkle with a little soy sauce and sesame seed oil. Stir in the linguine, mixing them evenly with the vegetables and return to the heat briefly, stirring and turning, until the linguine have reheated.

To serve

Roll the linguine and the julienne strips of vegetables around a fork and push off the fork onto individual heated plates, to form a "nest" for the pork chops. Surround with a trickle of the reduced marinade. Sprinkle with toasted sesame seeds.

This Chinese-inspired marinade goes very well with the delicate, tender flesh of veal chops, but they need careful attention while they are frying as the soy sauce and honey tend to make the surface of the chops caramelize and brown much more rapidly. Try to buy the more flavorsome farm-reared veal in preference to the bland and slightly "soggy" veal from milk-fed calves. Thin Chinese wheat noodles (fresh or dried) can be used instead of linguine.

Pork and shrimp kabobs and savory mango salad with herbs

For the kabobs

4 slices, 7 oz each, of boned
spare rib and/or bladebone
cut of pork
4 large shrimp, unpeeled
pinch of ground cumin
2 pinches of allspice
2 large scallions or fresh
white onions
peeled, crushed cloves from
2 heads of garlic
1 fresh chile pepper, seeded
and minced
½ bunch of fresh cilantro
2 tbsp olive oil
salt
8 wooden skewers or satay
sticks

For the mango salad

2 ripe, firm mangoes
½ fresh chile pepper, seeded
and crushed
chopped leaves from a small
bunch of fresh cilantro
juice of 1 lemon
1 tomato, blanched, peeled
(see method on p. 48),
seeded and diced
2 tbsp olive oil
salt, freshly ground pepper

For the tomato sauce

2 bright red, ripe tomatoes,
(see recipe on p. 54)
4 tbsp superfine sugar
2 tbsp rice wine vinegar
olive oil
harissa (optional)
salt, freshly ground pepper

Kabobs

Peel the shrimp, removing their heads and tail flippers. Place them on a large chopping board with the pork. Mince very finely with a very sharp, heavy knife. Add the spices, the onions, garlic (cut each clove in half and remove the central shoot if wished), chile and cilantro leaves, and finally some salt. Mix all these ingredients very thoroughly with your hands, to form a firm mass that sticks together. Divide in half and then in half again; each of these quantities needs to be divided in turn and shaped into 4 very firm balls or oval rissoles, yielding 16 in total. Thread 2 of these onto each skewer or satay stick and squeeze gently to secure.

Savory mango salad

Peel the mangoes with a very sharp serrated knife and cut off very thin slices. Cut the largest slices in half. Transfer to a bowl and mix with the crushed chile, cilantro leaves, lemon juice, and the finely diced tomatoes. Season with salt and pepper and set aside.

Tomato sauce

Crush the ripe tomato flesh. Press the flesh down into a strainer to extract all the juice. Heat the sugar until it forms a caramel and when this has darkened to a light brown color, add the rice wine vinegar and stir well. Add the tomato juice and reduce over a low heat until the mixture is much thicker and "syrupy," almost glossy in appearance. Season to taste, add a few drops of olive oil. You may wish to add a very little harissa if you like hot, peppery sauces.

Cooking the kabobs

Heat the olive oil over a high heat in a very wide, nonstick skillet and fry the kabobs until they are well browned and cooked through (turn them two or three times).

Serving the dish

Place 2 tablespoons of the mango salad on each plate and add 2 pork and shrimp kabobs. Hand round the tomato sauce separately in a pitcher or sauce boat.

> Pork and shrimp are very frequently combined in Southeast-Asian recipes; the Portuguese also love this combination and it is becoming increasingly popular in other western countries. These kabobs are very easy and rewarding to cook. To save time, you can use ¾ cup good quality commercially prepared tomato juice. Unless you like extremely hot tastes, it is advisable to remove the seeds from the chile peppers.

Adventures in faraway places: Asia, the Indian Ocean, the Islands

While the décor of Le Jardin des Sens—the Montpellier restaurant of La Compagnie des Comptoirs—draws on the East Indies for its inspiration, our restaurant on the beach at La Grande-Motte, the Effet Mer, evokes even more far-distant destinations. Here, too, there is a great, carved-wood door, admitting the visitor to an atmosphere of dreams and relaxation. The door is not surrounded by walls and it looks out, like the remnants of an ancient ark, over the dunes, toward a wide, horizontal marine landscape. In common with much of the furniture and woodwork, the door has traveled all the way from Bali. The paneling in the restaurant divides the space rhythmically into sections and the panels are decorated with carvings of flowers. Elsewhere, large antique beds, with draperies hanging from

Above: *the bar at La Compagnie des Comptoirs in Avignon unfolds like a drowned bamboo thicket, with a greenish light glowing between the stems. Facing page, left: the same tropical light filters through a green parasol sheltering the wares of a trader in the floating market in Bangkok.*

Below: *a sugar cane field in Martinique, photographed during the 1920s for the French colonial administration's records.*
Facing page, right: *coconut is an all-purpose ingredient in African, South-American, Indian and Indonesian cooking.*

their frameworks, await only the visitor's presence, ready to dispense repose surrounded by the wind, the sea, and the sun. The Moroccan *salon* provides shade, calm, and intimacy.

We have brought Morocco and Indonesia together in the same space, the better to express our love of travel in the widest sense, without ever remaining at a particular destination. What counts is the exoticism, luxury, and sensuality associated with everything that is far off, unfamiliar, and beautiful.

Harmonious marriages, subtle associations

The dishes we serve are in harmony with this principle, discernible in the ingredients and in the culinary techniques borrowed from the gastronomic traditions of Southeast Asia, China, Japan, and the many islands of that vast expanse of the world. Often these different styles share the same plate: a Thai papaya salad with *wasabi* (Japanese horseradish); an African favorite, plantain banana, with tempura; roast duck served with a red wine sauce—and with a date chutney as well; *nems*, the little Vietnamese version of spring rolls, served as a dessert with raspberries inside them and accompa-

Above: *green papayas and mangoes: these two fruits can be eaten before they are ripe; in Asia and in the West Indies they are used when still green, both raw and cooked, to make refreshing salads and as accompaniments to meat and fish dishes.*

nied by Italian mascarpone; Chinese litchis with a Basque liqueur, Izarra. We are not seeking to be provocative with these combinations of various dishes; they are the fruit of a meticulous search for harmony. This is the spirit that informs modern cooking, choosing from an ever-widening selection while trusting to what our senses and our discernment tell us.

Thailand remains one of the favorite sources of inspiration for our cooking. Thai dishes have such finesse, they are so delicately balanced, the variety of ingredients is so vast, and such is the subtlety of their tastes that they never cease to surprise us. Thai food exploits a wide range of sensations: the scale goes from extremely peppery—this is one of the world's hottest cuisines—to the soothing mildness provided by coconut milk, peanuts, green papaya, and rice. In the Thai repertoire of spices some tastes are as subtle as you will find anywhere: galangal, the leaves of the kaffir lime, lemon grass, the leaves and roots of fresh cilantro, complemented by chile peppers, limes, shrimp paste, and the fish sauce that is reminiscent of the ancient Romans' *garum*. We also team crustaceans such as large shrimp, crabs, and the smaller shrimp with Thailand's sweet and peppery sauces, or with Thai red, yellow, or green curry paste, and adopt the simple yet subtle method of cooking them gently, wrapped in banana leaves.

Japanese cooking is another of our points of reference. Here, the basic materials and foodstuffs make their presence felt more boldly and more simply, in a more straightforward manner. Salmon and tuna are prepared using the *tataki* method, just seared on the surface to seal them and then plunged into iced water to produce a dish that is at one and the same time robust, fresh, and light. The essence of this dish consists of the variety and originality of its cooking techniques, in the raw-cooked contrast, with the finishing touch of a full-bodied and aromatic soy sauce and a hint of *wasabi*.

The never-ending journey of the venturesome gourmet

Other dreams lead us to the Islands, those of the Pacific, of the Indian Ocean, and the Gulf of Mexico. The expression "the Islands" was once, and to a certain extent still is, synonymous with a bygone era and, hearing it, French people would immediately think of all those far-off parts of the world where the French traded in spices and cultivated crops on tropical plantations. France used to be heavily involved in trading in pepper from Zanzibar, cinnamon from Sri Lanka, and cassia wood from Borneo, cloves from the Moluccas, vanilla from Madagascar, Réunion, and Tahiti; allspice from Jamaica, dried orange peel from Haiti and Curaçao. Away from the islands, China was where French merchants traded in star anise and Sichuan pepper; West Africa supplied cardamoms and ginger, cocoa and cashew nuts. As for the countless varieties of capsicums and chile peppers in every shape, form, and strength, coconuts and fresh cilantro, these are available throughout the tropics.

Exotic fruits create a feast for the eyes and palate on one's plate and give a touch of refinement to desserts. They are always included in our *voyages gourmands*. The mango, which originated in Asia, has spread to most tropical regions and is a favorite, not only because of the tree's beauty but, more pertinently, for the sensual flavor and aroma of its fruit. Papaya is another tropical fruit that can be eaten when green, grated for refreshing salads in the cooking of Southeast Asia. When ripe the flesh is delicious sprinkled with lime juice. The pulp inside the passion fruit has a wonderful scent and taste which completely transforms desserts, while the pineapple, which has been known in France since the reign of Louis XIV three hundred years ago, remains one of our favorite fruits: we use it a great deal, in both savory and sweet dishes.

Above: *little fishing boats on the Pearl River, just off Macao, where for centuries the cooking has mirrored the region's racial diversity, blending the culinary traditions of China and Portugal.*

Crisp spring rolls with guinea fowl filling, papaya salad with cashew nuts, fresh cilantro

To serve 4

For the crisp spring rolls with guinea fowl filling
2 boned thighs of guinea fowl
2 tbsp soy-maple sauce (mix
½ tbsp soy sauce with 1½ tbsp
maple syrup)
4 wooden skewers or bamboo
satay sticks
2 spring roll wrappers (see
note at end of method)
1 egg yolk lightly beaten with
1 tsp cold water
4 cups oil for frying

For the papaya salad
1 under-ripe, firm papaya
1 tbsp lemon juice
3 tbsp olive oil
1 shallot, finely chopped
small bunch fresh cilantro
salt, freshly ground pepper

Garnish with
1 tbsp toasted, coarsely
chopped cashew nuts

Cut the guinea fowl flesh into large dice; marinate for 20 minutes in the soy sauce and maple syrup mixture. Take the leaves off the cilantro stalks and snip them coarsely.

Papaya salad

Peel the papaya and grate it (do not include any of dark seeds or their surrounding filaments). Season with salt and pepper and mix the grated papaya with the lemon juice, olive oil, and shallot. Add the cilantro shortly before serving.

Crisp spring rolls with guinea fowl filling

Drain off the marinade from the diced guinea fowl meat, pouring it into a small pan. Cook gently until it looks like a syrup; set aside. Cut the spring roll wrappers into rectangles that, when wrapped round the meat section of each brochette, will completely cover it. Dip the wooden skewers or satay sticks in cold water and then impale an even number of diced guinea fowl pieces on each one. Wrap the pieces of spring roll wrapper fairly tightly around the meat on the skewer; brush the edges and the long "side seam" of wrapper with beaten egg and press lightly to secure. Heat the oil until very hot (325 °F) and deep-fry the spring-roll-wrapped brochettes (use a frying basket if wished) until they are golden brown. Remove from the fryer and finish draining on paper towels.

To serve
Spoon the papaya salad onto small plates or into small bowls, sprinkle with the cashew nuts and place the brochettes on top; alternatively, serve as shown on facing page. Sprinkle each serving with a little of the reduced marinade.

Spring roll wrappers are sold in all Chinese food shops; do not use the rice flour Vietnamese spring roll (*nem*) wrappers which have to be moistened before use as they are not suitable for this dish.

Oriental pastry with pears, spiced syrup, and quince sorbet

For the quince sorbet

4 cups water

2¾ cups sugar

generous 1 lb cooked
quince flesh

For the spiced syrup

1 cup water

⅔ cup sugar

½ vanilla bean

½ cinnamon stick

2 star anise

1 scant tsp Sichuan
peppercorns

1 tbsp potato starch

For the pear pastry

1¾ stick/7 oz butter, softened
at room temperature
+ 1 stick/3½ oz butter, melted

1 cup superfine sugar +
4 tbsp for the phyllo sheets

2 eggs

2 cups ground almonds

3 pears

10 sheets of phyllo pastry
(see note on p. 34)

scant ½ cup chopped
pistachio nuts

⅔ cup chopped almonds

3½ tbsp clear, runny honey

To serve

extra spices (for decoration)

fresh mint

confectioners' sugar

164

Tastes of the Orient and colors of Asia

Quince sorbet

Make a syrup with the sugar and water: bring them to a boil and, when the sugar has completely dissolved, leave to cool.

Mix the cold, cooked quince flesh and the cold sugar syrup thoroughly; transfer this mixture to a sorbetière or ice-cream maker and freeze. Transfer to the freezer.

Spiced syrup

Mix the water, sugar, and the spices in a pan; bring to a boil and allow the sugar to dissolve completely. Have the potato starch ready mixed with approximately 2 tablespoons of cold water and stir into the syrup to thicken slightly. Cook while stirring over a very gentle heat for a few minutes. Remove from heat.

Pear pastry

Make the almond filling: beat the softened butter with 1 cup superfine sugar until pale and fluffy; beat in the eggs one at a time, then stir in the ground almonds. Set aside.

Peel the pears, cut them in half, remove the cores, and slice them thinly.

Preheat the oven to 325 °F.

Cut the phyllo sheets in half across their width; brush all the exposed surfaces with melted butter, using a soft pastry brush; use the extra 4 tbsp of superfine sugar to sprinkle over the butter-coated surfaces.

Using a large, nonstick baking sheet that will accommodate the phyllo sheets lying flat, place 5 of the buttered and sugar-sprinkled phyllo sheets on it, on top of one another; these layers will only have butter and sugar between them. Spread the egg, sugar, and almond mixture over the top layer and smooth it with a palette knife; place the sliced pears on top in

an even layer and sprinkle them with all the chopped pistachio nuts and half the almonds. Sprinkle as evenly as possible with the honey. Place the remaining phyllo sheets (brushed with butter and sprinkled with sugar) on top of the almond cream, nut, and honey layer. Sprinkle the top evenly with the remaining almonds. Bake for approximately 40 minutes. The surface of the pastry should be an even golden brown.

To serve

Cut the hot pastry into wide parallel strips and then into elongated triangles. Place 3 of these on each person's plate and sprinkle with some of the thickened spiced syrup.

Serve with a scoop of the quince sorbet. Decorate with spices (e.g. star anise), if wished, and with fresh mint leaves; dust lightly with sifted confectioners' sugar.

> We have added pears to our variation on the classic technique for baking *baklava*. Fruit adds a welcome fruity and slightly acid touch to the sweet pastry. This dessert combines crispness, melting softness, and spiciness; it is much better served warm than cold. Keep the remaining phyllo sheets well wrapped up in the refrigerator for later use.

"Trading Post" caramelized exotic fruits with spices, piña colada ice cream, Curaçao sauce

**For the caramelized
exotic fruits**
½ stick/2 oz butter
200 g (7 oz) superfine sugar
1 small, ripe pineapple
1 ripe papaya
1 ripe, firm mango
2 kiwi fruits
2 slightly under-ripe bananas
4 star anise
4 cinnamon sticks
2 vanilla beans
4 saffron pistils (or whole
saffron "threads")
4 twists of freshly milled
Sichuan pepper
scant 1 tsp spices for *pain
d'épices* (honey spice bread),
see note at end of method

For the Curaçao sauce
1½ cups Curaçao liqueur
scant ½ cup superfine sugar

**For the piña colada
ice cream**
10 egg yolks
⅔ cup superfine sugar
2 cups pineapple pulp (see
note at end of method)
2 cups canned coconut milk
scant ½ cup Jamaica rum

Piña colada ice cream

Start preparation the day before you plan to serve this. Beat the egg yolks with the superfine sugar until very pale and frothy; the mixture should form a "ribbon" when the whisk is lifted above the bowl. Bring the pineapple pulp and coconut milk to a boil together in a pan, remove from the heat and stir gently into the sugar and egg mixture; return this to the pan (or use a large double boiler) and cook over a gentle heat (or over simmering water) until the mixture reaches a temperature of 185 °F (it should just thicken slightly); do not allow it to come close to boiling at any point. Pour into a large, lipped bowl and stir in the rum. Chill in the refrigerator for 24 hours. Process in the ice-cream maker 30 minutes before serving.

"Trading Post" spiced exotic fruits

Peel and prepare all the fruits and cut them into pieces of your preferred size and shape. Heat the butter in a very large, deep pan. Add the sugar and the following spices, just as they are, without grinding or crumbling them: star anise, cinnamon sticks, and the vanilla beans (which should be slit lengthwise and the seeds and beans both added to the pan); lastly, add the saffron. Add all the fruit and cook over a moderate heat, just long enough for them to heat through and be coated with the light caramel. While they are cooking, sprinkle with the freshly ground Sichuan pepper and *pain d'épices* spice mixture.

Curaçao sauce

Mix the Curaçao and the sugar in a heavy-bottomed pan; reduce over a moderate heat until it becomes syrupy. Leave to cool.

Assembling the dessert

Arrange a selection of the warm or cold spiced fruits on each dish. Place a scoop of the piña colada ice cream to one side and drizzle the Curaçao sauce over it; trickle a thin ribbon of the sauce around the serving of fruits as well.

To make your pineapple pulp, simply place the peeled and cored flesh in a food processor or blender and process until smooth. If you have to use tinned pineapple, drain it well beforehand. *Pain d'épices* (spiced honey bread) mixture is blended, using ground spices, as follows: 2 tsp ground cinnamon, 1 tsp ground (powdered) ginger, 1 tbsp ground fresh, green (or dried) anise seeds, 1 tsp ground nutmeg, 1 tsp ground cloves. Mix well and sprinkle a pinch over each serving. You may prefer to grind the whole spices in a coffee grinder for a fresh mixture. Keep what is left over in an airtight jar. The Sichuan peppercorns must be freshly ground in a pepper mill.

Caramelized pineapple and lemon grass brochettes, exotic fruit and orange-flower water sauce

For the pineapple brochettes
4–6 dried apricots
2 tbsp seedless raisins
orange-flower water (for soaking the dried fruit)
1 large pineapple, not too ripe
2 lemon grass stalks and bulbs
4 tbsp superfine sugar
¼ stick/1 oz unsalted butter

For the exotic fruit sauce
⅓ cup ripe apricot flesh (puréed)
⅓ cup ripe peach or nectarine flesh (puréed)
1 cup fresh passion fruit pulp, sieved, or juice
½ cup unsweetened mango juice (or puréed flesh)
1 vanilla bean (slit to release the seeds)
1 cinnamon stick
2 star anise

Exotic fruit sauce

Place all the fruit and fruit juices in a pan with the spices. Bring slowly to a boil. Remove from the heat, cover tightly, and leave to stand for the flavors to develop.

Caramelized pineapple brochettes

Place the apricots and the raisins in a small, deep bowl or cup and add sufficient orange-flower water to cover them completely. Leave to soften and flavor.

Peel and core the pineapple and cut in quarters. Remove the outermost layer of the lemon grass and slice off the very top of the stem at a very slanting angle. Cut the lemon grass lengthwise in half. Thread the chunks of pineapple onto these lemon grass "skewers," pushing the sharp, freshly cut end in first. Heat the butter and sugar in a wide, nonstick skillet until the sugar has completely dissolved; add the "brochettes" of pineapple and cook them over a moderate heat, turning 3 times so that all the exposed surfaces caramelize. As soon as they are golden brown all over, add the exotic fruit juice to the pan and continue cooking, still uncovered, for up to 10 minutes over a gentle heat.

To serve

Transfer to deep dessert plates or bowls and surround with the soaked dried fruits and juices.

> You may wish to add an extra, exotic touch by cooking and/or serving this dish in an earthenware *tajine*, typical of Moroccan cooking. In France *pêches de vigne* (red-fleshed peaches grown among the vines) are used for this recipe. Choose the best quality, plump, moist dried fruits you can buy. The use of lemon grass adds an unexpected Southeast-Asian flavor to this dessert. The pineapple should be just ripe; it will soften during cooking.

Poached litchis, granita of Izarra liqueur, iced water flavored with lemon verbena

To serve 6

For the poached litchis
4 cups water
1 cup sugar
20 litchis (peeled and pitted)

For the Izarra granita
4 cups water
2¾ cups superfine sugar
2 cups Perrier water
¾ cups green Izarra liqueur

**For the iced water
flavored with lemon
verbena**
4 cups Perrier water
1 cup sugar
small bunch fresh or dried
lemon verbena

For decorating the dessert
A few fresh lemon verbena
leaves
coarsely chopped pistachio
nuts

Poached litchis

Bring the sugar and water to a boil in a pan; when the sugar has completely dissolved, add the peeled, pitted litchis and poach them for 5 minutes. Allow to cool; when cold, chill in the refrigerator, in the cooking syrup.

Granita of Izarra liqueur

Mix the sugar and water until the sugar has dissolved completely (do not heat). Stir in all the remaining ingredients and pour into a rectangular freezer-proof container. Place in the freezer. When the time comes to serve the granita, break up the frozen mixture into ice granules by scraping the tines of a strong fork along the surface.

Iced water flavored with lemon verbena

Bring the Perrier water and the sugar to a boil. Add the lemon verbena, cover, and leave to infuse for 15 minutes, away from the heat. Pour through a fine-mesh strainer and, when cool, refrigerate.

To serve

Spoon the granita into glass coupes or small bowls, sprinkle with the lemon verbena iced water. Place the drained litchis on top of the granita and sprinkle with some chopped pistachios. Decorate with a fresh lemon verbena leaf.

In this dessert a Chinese fruit and Izarra liqueur (its taste reminiscent of sage and rosemary, made in the French Pyrenees, in the Basque country) combine their very refreshing tastes, accentuated by the use of lemon verbena. This is an ideal dessert to serve at the end of a rich meal.

Tastes of the Orient and colors of Asia

Carrot "ravioli" with lime custard cream filling, vanilla sauce, and lemon balm

4 very large, fresh, preferably
organic carrots
1 cup superfine sugar
2 cups water

For the lime custard cream
5 egg yolks
scant ½ cup superfine sugar
2 cups heavy cream
finely grated zest of 2 limes

For the vanilla sauce
1 cup water
2 tbsp superfine sugar
½ vanilla bean
1 tbsp potato starch

To serve
shredded fresh lemon balm
leaves

Lime custard cream
The day before you plan to serve this dish, complete this first preparation stage for the lime cream. Beat the egg yolks with the sugar until pale and very creamy; fold in the cream and the grated lime zest. Chill in the refrigerator for 24 hours.

Carrots
These should be prepared on the day the dish is to be served. Peel and trim the carrots; slice them very thinly into rounds, using a mandoline or a very sharp knife. You will only use the large rounds of carrot. Bring the water and sugar to a boil, add the carrots and cook them over a gentle heat for 15 minutes. Leave to cool completely.

Vanilla sauce
Bring the water and sugar to a boil with the vanilla bean and its seeds, having first scraped these out into the water. Mix the potato starch with a little cold water and add sufficient to thicken the vanilla-flavored liquid a little; stir while cooking over a gentle heat for a few minutes. Remove from heat.

Cooking and assembling the dessert
Preheat the oven to 195 °F. Strain the lime cream through a strainer and pour it into a shallow, nonstick baking pan or ceramic dish. Place the pan or dish into the oven and bake for 1 hour. Remove from the oven and allow to cool.

Drain the carrot slices. Use a very small-diameter pastry cutter to cut out rounds of the lime cream custard. Place 3 carrot slices on each plate; use a spatula to remove the custard shapes from the dish carefully and place one on top of each carrot slice. Place a second carrot slice on top of each piece of lime custard cream. Sprinkle with the vanilla-flavored sauce and decorate with shredded fresh lemon balm leaves.

Carrots are used in sweet dishes in several parts of the world (in carrot halva in India and in carrot cake in the United States). In this recipe, cooking them in sugar syrup gives them added sweetness. This is quite a complicated dessert and calls for some dexterity but your guests will find it intriguing and delicious.

Frozen chocolate mousse, lemon-flavored almond brittle, whipped yogurt

To serve 12

12 tart rings, 2½ inches in diameter

For the chocolate mousse

1 cup sugar syrup at 85 °F:
1½ cups superfine sugar
and 2 cups water
8 egg yolks
9 oz couverture chocolate
containing at least 64%
cocoa solids (see note)
3½ tbsp whipping cream,
whisked until stiff

For the lemon almond brittle

17 oz almond brittle
1 tbsp pure lemon essence

For the tuiles

1 stick/4 oz butter, softened at
room temperature
scant ½ cup superfine sugar
scant ½ cup cassonade
(raw, unrefined cane sugar)
scant ½ cup orange juice
⅔ all-purpose flour

For the chocolate coating

9 oz dark couverture
chocolate (see note at
end of method)
9 oz cocoa butter

Serving and decoration

2 cups thick Greek-style
yogurt
whole milk
pure cocoa powder

Chocolate mousse

Bring the syrup to a boil over a gentle heat. Use a stand mixer, with the large bowl in place and fit the whisk attachment. Beat the egg yolks until they are very creamy; keep the whisk attachment rotating at high speed and pour the syrup onto the eggs in a thin, continuous stream. Keep beating until the mixture has cooled completely. While this is in progress, melt the chocolate over hot water or in the microwave oven and stir into the cooled egg and sugar mixture. Fold in 1 tablespoon of the stiffly beaten cream, then fold in the remaining cream.

Lemon almond brittle

Break up the almond brittle or praline into small pieces and add just enough very hot water to melt it, forming a thick sauce. Heat gently in a heavy-bottomed pan if necessary. Stir in the lemon essence.

Tuiles

Preheat the oven to 350 °F. Beat the butter and sugar until pale and creamy; stir in the cassonade sugar, followed by the orange juice. Sift in the flour and fold into the mixture. Have ready a baking sheet covered with silicone baking paper or nonstick wax paper. Spread the mixture out as evenly as possible over the paper and bake in the oven until it is very pale golden brown. Working quickly, while the sheet is still hot, cut it into fairly large triangles and wrap these hot triangles around a rolling pin or similarly shaped utensil. Leave to cool.

Assembling and serving

Place the tart rings on a nonstick baking sheet and fill with the chocolate mixture; freeze until solid. Use a sharp-edged teaspoon to scoop out a small depression in the center of each and, using a pastry bag and nozzle, fill with some of the lemon almond brittle sauce. Mask this addition with a thin layer of the scooped-out chocolate mixture. Return to the freezer. Make the chocolate coating: melt the chocolate with the cocoa butter over hot water in a double boiler or in the microwave oven. Take the chocolate mousse rounds out of their molds and coat with the melted chocolate mixture as evenly as possible. Place in the refrigerator.

Beat the Greek-style yogurt with a little milk, until it barely holds its shape. Place a frozen chocolate mousse in the center of each plate. Put a tuile on top to decorate. Surround with the yogurt. Sift a little cocoa powder around the edge of the dish.

If you cannot buy *couverture* chocolate (see note on page 110), buy the best baker's chocolate (*chocolat patissier*) that you can find, with the highest possible cocoa solids content. Menier dark chocolate, preferably unsweetened, is a suitable substitute. You may find coating the chocolate mousse rounds with chocolate difficult; in a professional kitchen, this is done with a special spray-gun utensil. Alternatively, dust the rounds with a little cocoa powder.

White chocolate and coconut ice cream, caramel popsicles, chocolate sauce

To serve 6

For the coconut dacquoise base

Preheat the oven to 350 °F.

Whisk the egg whites until stiff, add the superfine sugar and continue beating until the meringue is very firm. Keep whisking as you add the grated coconut, the confectioners' sugar, and finally the sifted flour. Spread the meringue mixture out on a sheet of nonstick wax paper on a baking sheet in an even layer approximately ¾ inch deep. Smooth the surface with a palette knife and bake in the oven for 15 minutes or until the dacquoise meringue is firm. Transfer to a rack and leave to cool.

When cold, use a 3-inch pastry cutter to cut out rounds.

White chocolate and coconut ice

Beat the whipping cream until it stands up in firm peaks. Break the white chocolate up into very small, evenly sized pieces and place in a large mixing bowl. Heat the coconut milk until almost boiling and pour it over the white chocolate; mix well with a spatula until the mixture is very smooth. Stir in the Malibu liqueur and keep stirring continuously as the mixture cools to lukewarm: fold in the whisked cream. Transfer the white chocolate and coconut milk mixture to dome-shaped moulds (*mini-bombes*), preferably flexible; ideally, these should have a diameter of 3 inches so that they will sit neatly on top of the meringue rounds. Freeze the white chocolate ice cream "bombes." When they have frozen hard, melt the dark chocolate. Turn the white chocolate "domes" out of their molds and cover them with the melted chocolate (do this after anchoring them to the meringue bases with a dab of the melted chocolate). Transfer to the refrigerator.

Caramel-coconut popsicles

Break open the coconut and scrape off the thin brownish inner layer. Cut out the white flesh and grate it finely. Using a small ice-cream scoop, shape 12 small balls of caramel ice cream. Push a popsicle stick securely into each ball and return to the freezer. Take them out of the freezer, check that the sticks are securely frozen in place and roll them in the grated coconut. Return to the freezer again.

Chocolate sauce

Bring the water and sugar to a boil to make a syrup. Stir in the cocoa powder thoroughly; cook for 5 minutes and then stir in the butter. Chill in the refrigerator.

Assembling the dessert

Place a frozen chocolate mousse on its base of meringue in the center of each plate; add 2 popsicles and a trickle of the chocolate sauce.

> You will need to work out a timetable when preparing this dessert: the finished ice-cream bombes should not have to wait too long in the refrigerator, but they should not be served deep-frozen, rock-hard. The refrigerator ice box can be used as a halfway house if needed.

For the coconut
dacquoise
1 lb egg whites
(approximately 14 medium-sized egg whites)
1 generous cup superfine sugar
1 lb freshly grated coconut
2 cups confectioners' sugar
⅔ cup all-purpose flour

For the frozen chocolate and coconut milk mousses
2 cups whipping cream
11 oz white chocolate
½ cup fresh or canned coconut milk
½ cup Malibu liqueur (rum and coconut milk flavor)
7 oz dark, best quality cooking chocolate

For the coconut-coated caramel ice-cream popsicles
1 coconut
4 cups best quality caramel ice cream
12 popsicle sticks

For the chocolate sauce
1 cup water
¾ cup superfine sugar
¾ cup pure cocoa powder
¼ stick/1 oz unsalted butter

Fritters with sweet pumpkin filling, ice cream, lemon rosemary sauce

To serve 8–10

4 cups oil for frying

For the brioche dough
1 oz fresh yeast
a little warm milk
4 cups all-purpose white flour
4 tbsp superfine sugar
scant 1 tsp salt
5 eggs
2¼ sticks/9 oz butter, at room temperature
1 egg, beaten with 2 tsps cold water, to glaze

For the pumpkin filling
2 cups pumpkin flesh
2 cups water
½ cup milk
scant ½ cup superfine sugar

For the ice cream
6 cups whole-cream milk
5 tbsp superfine sugar

For the rosemary and lemon sauce
2 lemons
2 cups water
1½ cups superfine sugar
1 sprig of fresh rosemary

To assemble and decorate
superfine sugar for dusting the fritters
1 dessertspoon of ground cinnamon

Sweet yeast bun dough

Mix the yeast with a little warm milk. Leave to stand for 5 minutes.

Sift the flour with the sugar and salt into a large mixing bowl, forming a mound. Make a well in the center and into it pour the yeast solution and the eggs. Use your hand to stir and incorporate all the ingedients; knead the dough until it is smooth, elastic, and comes away from the sides of the bowl. If you have a large electric mixer with a dough hook you can knead the dough mechanically.

Add the butter, cut into small pieces, and work this into the dough. Leave to "rest" for about 30 minutes, then knead again (if using a mixer, do this at medium speed). When the dough forms a ball and leaves the sides of the bowl cleanly, place in a large, clean bowl in a warm (not hot) place and leave to rise for 1½ hours. When the dough has doubled in size, knock it down again. Wrap it in plastic food wrap and chill in the least cold part of the refrigerator.

Sweet pumpkin filling

Cook the pumpkin flesh for approximately 20 minutes in the boiling water, milk, and sugar. Drain well and reduce to a thick purée, adding a little of the cooking liquid if it is too thick to process until smooth. Chill in the refrigerator.

Ice cream

Mix the milk and sugar in a pan. Heat and simmer until reduced to 2 cups. Chill overnight, then freeze in an ice-cream maker.

Rosemary and lemon sauce

Peel the lemons with a very sharp serrated knife or patent peeler. Cook the lemons with the sugar and water for 1 hour over a gentle heat. Drain the lemons and process them until smooth in the blender, adding some of the warm syrup to make a pouring sauce. Add the rosemary. Chill in the refrigerator.

Frying the fritters

Take a pastry bag and smooth nozzle and fill two-thirds full with the pumpkin puree. Divide the sweet yeast dough in half. Roll out one half into a sheet approximately ⅛ inch thick and brush the entire upper surface with the egg yolk and water mixture. Pipe "blobs" of purée on the dough sheet. Roll out the remaining dough into a sheet and use it to cover the first sheet. Use a finger to press very lightly around the mounds to make the dough sheets stick together. Using a 2-inch diameter plain pastry cutter cut out little "pies" of dough and filling. Leave to rest for 15 minutes while heating the frying oil to 325 °F. Fry the fritters until they are golden brown.

To serve

Roll the drained fritters in the superfine sugar, previously mixed with the ground cinnamon. Serve while hot, accompanied by the ice cream in separate glass dishes and hand the sauce round separately.

These quantities are large, assuming that you will be making these fritters for a special occasion, such as a child's birthday party. If you are catering for 5–6 people, for a dessert, halve these quantities.

Appendices

List of recipes by chapter

Tastes of the Orient and colors of Asia   p. 119

Index of recipes

Photographic credits

All the photographs in this book were taken by Bernhard Winkelman with the following exceptions:
Olivier Maynard: p. 6, 7, 12, 14 (below right & above left), 16-17, 27, 58-59, 118-119.
Olivier Thieule: Cover image (front flap), p. 11.
Didier Barthélémy: p. 14 (above right).
Marc Walter: p. 44, 47, 91, 161.
Vérascopes Richard-Photothèque Hachette: p. 28, 74, 93, 103, 134, 158.
Agence Top: p. 43 (Jean-Daniel Sudres), 73 (Christine Fleurent).
Agence Rapho: p. 26 (Xavier Desmer), 101 (R. & S. Michaud), 133 (Gérard Sioen),
157 (Mike Yamashita).
Copyright: p. 2-3.

Acknowledgments

Jacques & Laurent Pourcel and Olivier Château would like to thank the following:
Thierry for all the time he spent compiling the recipes.
Valérie and Bernard for their time and their creativity.
Christophe for creating the desserts for their photo call!
Denis, Élie, Ruddy, Nicolas and Nathalie for their indispensable help.
A particular mention for our good friend Philippe Lamboley, for launching the project.
Sophie, Marie-Pierre, Catherine, Brigitte…well done, girls!
Xav and Fred…Keep going…there's still a long way ahead of us!
Our thanks also go to Stephen and to everyone who believes in us!

Valérie Lhomme's is very grateful to the Lluck boutique in Montpellier, AZA (faiences – china and earthenware) and Reine de Saba for all their kind help.

The editor would like to thank Madame Figaro magazine for allowing us to reproduce the photograph on page 85 and also thanks Charlotte Buch-Muller for her invaluable help and her meticulous checking of the text.

Printed in Singapore by Tien Wah Press